LEARN FRENCH IN 30 DAYS THROUGH ENGLISH

Bhavna Chopra

DIAMOND BOOKS

ISBN : 978-81-288-2130-1

Published by : **Diamond Pocket Books Pvt. Ltd.**
X-30, Okhla Industrial Area, Phase-II
New Delhi-110020
Phone : 011-41611861, 40712100
Fax : 011-41611866
E-mail : sales@dpb.in
Website : www.dpb.in
Edition : 2021

Learn French in 30 days through English
By: Bhavna Chopra

Dedicated

to

my beloved father.

INTRODUCTION TO FRENCH

The French language is descended from Latin and first appeared in writing in 842 AD when it was used in the Strasbourg Oaths. Before then Latin was the language used for literature throughout Europe. Universally after English French is the second language spoken in 33 countries. French is the main language of France and is spoken in other countries like Canada, Belgium, Luxembourg, Lebanon, French Guinea, French Pacific territories. The prehistory of the French language begins with the colonization of Gaul by the Romans. Sound of this language is very soft and sharp, so it is called as "Language of Romance".

People often wonder how many French speakers there are, but a definitive answer is not easy to find. In 1999, French was the 11th most common first language in the world, with 77 million first language speakers and another 51 million second language speakers, according to the Ethnologue Report. (1) French is the second most commonly-taught second language in the world (after English).

Another source, *La Francophonie dans le monde 2006-2007* (2), looks at it differently:

- 128 million Francophones: speak French (as a native or adopted language) fluently and use it on a regular basis.
- 72 million "*partiol*" Francophones: live in a francophone country but do not speak French regularly, due to limited knowledge.
- 100-110 million students of all ages: do not live in a francophone country, but have learned/are learning French in order to communicate with Francophones.

This book is designed for beginners in such a way that they can learn language in 30 days and the speciality of this book is while learning n obvious reason to learn a new language is to be able to communicate with the people who speak it. This includes both the people you meet when traveling as well as people in your own community. Your trip to another country will be greatly enhanced in both ease of communication and friendliness if you speak the language. Speaking another's language shows respect for that culture, and people in every country prefer it when tourists make an effort to speak the local language, even if all you can say in it is "hello" and "please." In addition, learning another language can also help you to communicate with local immigrant populations at home.

Cultural understanding

Speaking a new language helps you to get to know another people and culture, as language and culture go hand in hand. Because language simultaneously defines and is defined by the world around us, learning another language opens one's mind to new ideas and new ways of looking at the world.

For example, the fact that many languages have more than one translation of "you" indicates that these languages (and the cultures that speak them) place a greater emphasis on distinguishing between audiences than does English. French distinguishes between *tu* (familiar) and *vous* (formal/plural), while Spanish has five words that indicate one of four categories: familiar/singular (*tú* or *vos*, depending on the country), familiar/plural (*vosotros*), formal/singular (*Ud.*), and formal/plural (*Uds.*). Meanwhile, Arabic distinguishes between *nta* (masculine singular), *nti* (feminine singular), and *ntuma* (plural). In contrast, English uses "you" for masculine, feminine, familiar, formal, singular, and plural. The fact that these languages have such different ways of looking at "you" indicates cultural differences between the people who speak them: French and Spanish focus on familiarity vs formality, while Arabic emphasizes gender. This is just one example of many of the linguistic and cultural differences between languages.

In addition, when you speak another language, you can enjoy literature, film, and music in the original language. It is extremely difficult for a translation to be a perfect replica of the original; the best way to understand what the author really meant is to read what the author actually wrote.

Business and careers

Speaking more than one language is a skill which will increase your marketability. Schools and employers tend to prefer candidates who speak one or more foreign languages. Even though English is widely spoken in much of the world, the fact is that the global economy depends on communication. When dealing with France, for example, someone who speaks French will have an obvious advantage over someone who doesn't.

Language enhancement

Learning another language can help you to understand your own. Many languages have contributed to the development of English, so learning those will teach you where words and even grammatical structures are from, and augment your vocabulary to boot. Also, in learning how another language differs from your own, you will increase your understanding of your own language. For many people, language is innate - we know how to say something, but we don't necessarily know why we say it that way. Learning another language can change that.

Each subsequent language you study will be, in some respects, a little easier, because you've already learned how to learn another language. Plus, if the languages are related, such as French and Spanish, German and Dutch, or Arabic and Hebrew, some of what you've already learned will apply to the new language as well, making the new language that much easier, you will also being introduced by the culture of France. Explanation in this book is very simple and comprehensible. You will fimd the pronunciation of each and every word in English which help you to learn French pronunçiation.

This look is only meant for the beginners to learn basic french which is being used in daily life.It is advisable to read each chapter daily and understand each chapter thoroughly, if the concepts are not clear then don't jump on the next chapter.

There are total 30 chapters and at the end of this book you will also be familiar with the conversation and proverbs which are used in general by French.

The vocabulary is strictly limited to French words and expressions that are in common use. Explanation of all the tenses are so simple to understand.

How the book is organized

Learn French in 30 days contains:

- 30 lessons
- Alphabets and their pronunciation
- Numbers and writing sstyle
- Grammar
- Verbs
- Tenses
- Colours
- Dresses

- Household items
- Each lesson has the exercise and the "test yourself".
- conversations
- Description of the object with the help of pictures.
- Consists day to day use of phrases.
- Proverbs

In French also there are 26 alphabets, 5 are vowels a, e, i, o, u and the others are consonants. In French, there are few accents which are only used in vowels and when they are used on the vowels they change the sound of the word.

French accent

Symbol	**French accent**
'	**accent grave**
'	**accent aigu**
^	**accent circonflexe**
Ç	**cedilla**
Ë	**accent trema**
Œ	**o e ligature**
Æ	**a e ligature**

To type these accent, French keyboard is not required, you can type these characters by using the following formula.

Accent	**Formula**	**accents on the vowels**
'	ctrl +'	a , e and u
'	ctrl+ '	a and e
^	ctrl+shift+^	over all the vowels
Trema	ctrl+shift+;:	e and o
o e ligature	ctrl+shift&	press o
a e ligature	ctrl+shift+&	press a

Contents

Le Leçon 1

French Alphabets – l'alphabet en Français

In French there are 5 vowels and 21 consonants which make as total 26 alphabets. Alphabets written in French will be same as in English, only the difference is in the pronunciation, though there are few alphabets which are pronounced same as in English. A, E, I, O, U are the vowels and the remainders are consonants,remember "H" is always silent in French.

Alphabets in English	Pronunciation in French	As pronounced in English
A	aa	*as "a " in army*
B	be	*as "b" In baby*
C	ce	*as "c" in same*
D	de	*as "th" in mother*
E	a	*as "a" in along*
F	ef	*as "af" in Africa*
G	gee	*as "s" in measure*
H	al	*it is always silent*
I	I	*as "e" in English*
J	zee	*as "zea" in zeal*
K	ka	*as "cal" in calm*
L	l	*as "l" in english*
M	em	*as "am"in amplifier*
N	en	*as "n" in nest*
O	o	*as "o" in old*
P	pe	*as "pai" in paint*
Q	k	*as "co" in come*
R	not equivalent – It Is pronounced at the back of the throat	
S	es	*as "s" in std*
T	te	*as "t" in Pakistan*
U	eu	*as "eu" in english*
V	ve	*as "vei" in Vietnam*
W	dublave	*as "w " water*
X	iks	*as "x" in six*
Y	y	*as "y" in y*
Z	zed	*as "z" in z*

Numbers

Cardinal numbers and Ordinal numbers

Spellings of the numbers written in French are totally different like pronunciation.

Cardinal numbers

Numbers	Spellings	As pronounced in English
0	zero	*as ze in zebra and as ho in home=ze+ho*
1	un	*as u in uncle*
2	deux	*the*
3	trois	*thua*
4	quatre	*cath*
5	cinq	*sunk*
6	seize	*cease*
7	sept	*set*
8	huit	*wheat*
9	neuf	*nuf*
10	dix	*this*
11	onze	*as as on in onion and as z in zebra=on+z*
12	douze	*dooz*
13	treize	*threz*
14	quatorze	*cathorze*
15	quinze	*canze*
16	seize	*sez*
17	dix-sept	*this+set*
18	dix-huit	*this+wheat*
19	dix-neuf	*this+nef*
20	vingt	*as w in won*
21	vingt et un	*w +te+ u =w+te+un*
22	vingt deux	*w+the*
23	vingt trois	*w+thua*
24	vingt quatre	*w+cath*
30	trente	*thront*
31	trente et un	*thront+te+un*
32	trente deux	*thront+the*
40	quarante	*khonte*

41	quarante et un	***khonte+te+un***
50	cinquante	***sunkonte***
51	cinquante et un	***sunkonte+te+un***
60	soixante	***suasont***
61	soixante et un	***suasont+te+un***
70	soixante dix	***suasont+te+this***
71	soixante et onze (60 +11)	***suasont+te+on+z***
72	soixante douze(60+12)	***suasont+te+dooz***
80	quatre-vingt	***cath+w***
81	quatre-vingt-et-un	***as already explained***
82	quatre-vingt-deux	***as already explained***
90	quatre-vingt-dix (80+10)	***as already explained***
91	Quatre-vingt-douze(80+11)	***as already explained***
100	Cent	***so***
101	cent un	***as already explained***
200	deux cent	***deux so***
1000	mille	***meel***

Ordinal numbers

Numbers	French spellings	As pronounced in English
1	premier	***prhomeer***
2	deuxième	***dzeeyeme***
3	troisième	***thusazeeyeme***
4	quatrième	***catheeyeme***
5	cinquième	***sunkeeyem***
6	sixième	***seezeyeme***
7	septième	***seteeyem***
8	huitième	***wheateeyem***
9	neuvième	***nveeyem***
10	dixième	***thiseeyem***
11	onzième	***onzeeyem***
12	douzième	***doozeeyem***
13	treizième	***thrzeeyem***
14	quatorzième	***cathzeeyem***
15	quinzième	***canzeeyem***
16	seizième	***seezeeyem***
17	dix-septième	***deezsetieme***
18	dix-huitième	***distieme***
19	dix-neuvième	***disneveeyem***
20	vingtième	***vinteeyem***

21	vingt-et-unième	***vinteeyem***
22	vingt deuxième	***vingdeezeeyem***
60	soixantième	***susanteeyem***
61	soixante-et-unième	***susanteeyem***
70	soixante-dixième	***susantdeezeeyem***
80	quatre-vingtième	***cathvinteeyem***

Note: when writing number in French, the function of periods and commas is reversed from the english function. Commas are used in decimals and periods in numbers of four or more digits. Thus 1,000-one thousand becomes 1.000-mille in French and 1.5 is translated as 1.5-un virgule cinq.

L'exercise

A. Ecriez en numéro

1) Quatre vingt neuf ***(cathr w neuf)***
2) Vingt-et-un ***(e te un)***
3) Trente trios ***(thront thua)***
4) Cinquante six ***(sunkonte seez)***
5) Quatre vingt treize ***(cathre w threize)***
6) deux cent dix ***(the so dees)***

B. Write in words

1) 95
2) 138
3) 189
4) 34
5) 564
6) 876

Answers :

A.1) 89, 2)21 3)33 4)56 5)93 6)210

B.1) quatre cinquante ***(cathre sunkonte)***
2) cent trente huit, ***(so thront wheat)***
3) cent quatre vingt neuf ***(so cathre w nuf)***
4) trente quatre ***(thront cathre)***
5) cinq cent soixante quatre ***(sunk so suasont cathre)***
6) huit cent soixante seize. ***(wheat so suasont sez)***

Le Leçon 2

Subject Pronouns

The **subject** of a sentence is the person or thing which performs the action. **Subject pronouns** replace this person or thing.

Forms	Singular	As pronounced in English
I	Je	J
You	Tu	Tue
He / She	Il/Elle	Eel / L
We	Nous	Nooz
You	Vous	Vooz
They	Ils/ Elles	Eel / L

Note : Tu is used when speaking to children, animals or close friends and relatives.

Vous is used when speaking to more than one person, or to someone you don't know or who is older.

On can be translated into English as one, the people, we, they or you.

Tutoyer and **vousvoyer** are two verbs that have no direct translation into English. Tutoyer means to use tu or be informal with someone, while vousvoyer means to use vous or be informal with someone.

Ils - If there is a group of boys or group of both boys and girls

Elles – If they is a group of girls

Greetings

When greeting someone in French, you should make sure that the expression you use corresponds to the relationship you have with that person.

Bonjour and **au revoir** can be used with everyone

Salut is much more informal and frequently used by young people, friends or members of the same family.

How would you say "hello" to :

(a) Hi Pierre, an old friend – Salut Pierre ***(salu peeh)***
(b) A lady, Unknown person – Bonjour Madam (***bonju madam***)
(c) Your boss – Bonjour, Monsieur ***(bonju maunseyeur)***

How would you say "Goodbye" to :

a. Hi Pierre, an old friend – Salut Pierre ***(saloo peeh)***

b. A lady, Unknown person – Au revoir Madam ***(avwah madam)***

c. Your boss – Au revoir, Monsieur ***(avwah maunseeyeur)***

Basic Greetings

Pierre - Bonjour Stephanie. ***(bonju stephanie)***
Stephanie – Bonjour ***(bonju)***
Pierre – Comment çava? ***(kamo sava)***
Stephanie- çava bien, merci / je suis très bien et toi?
(cava beea, mehsi / je suee thre beea a tua)
Pierre – très bien. ***(thre beea)***
Stephanie- Au revoir. ***(awah)***

Some basic phrases

(1)	Goodnight	Bonnuit	(***bon nuee)***
(2)	Goodafternoon	Bon aprèsmidi	***(bonapreemidhi)***
(3)	Thanks a lot,	merci beaucoup	***(merci bucou)***
(4)	Welcome!	de rien –l	***(the riyah)***
(5)	Have a nice day!	Bonjournèe	***(bonjournee)***
(6)	See you later!	A tout á l'heure / A plus tard	***(a tut a l h / a plu tahrd)***
(7)	See you soon!	A bientôt!	***(abheeyanto)***
(8)	Excuse me!	Pardon	***(pakhdo)***
(9)	Lets go !	Allons-y	***(aalo zee)***
(10)	Nice to meet you!	Enchanté(e)!	***(enshantee)***
(11)	Of course!	Bien sûr!	***(beeyan sur***)
(12)	Here it is	Voila	***(voila)***
(13)	What / Pardon please	Comment!	***(kamo***)

Le Leçon 3

Verbs

A verb is the action word in a sentence. It is the word that says what happens, discusses an action, or describes a state of being. French verbs must be conjugated (inflected).

There are 2 forms of verbs which are mainly used in French, without which sentences can not be framed , Avoir means " to be " and Être means " to have ", will learn more on French verbs later.

Avoir-Avoir means "to have" in most senses, including having in one's possession and currently experiencing

Person	Singular(pronuncitation)	Plural
1st	Je suis***(Suee)***	Nous sommes***(nooz zom)***
2 nd	Tu as ***(a)***	Vous êtes(***voozet)***
3rd	Il/Elle a ***(a)***	Ils/Elles sont (***L , eelzo)***

Être - Être is one of the most common French verbs. It is irregular in conjugation and literally means «to be.» Être is also used in some common idiomatic expressions.

Person	Singular(Pronunciation)	Plural
1st	J'ai***(je)***	Nous avons ***(noozavo)***
2 nd	Tu es***(a)***	Vous avez ***(voozave)***
3rd	Il/Elle est ***(a)***	Ils/Elles ont ***(L, eelzo)***

Examples :

Je suis le professeur	***(je suee le profeseuer)***
Tu as Indien ?	***(tu a andien)***
Il est mon ami.	***(eel a maun amee)***
Elle est très gentil.	***(l a thre jentil)***
J'ai le stylo	***(je le steelo)***

Negative sentences :

In framing the negative sentence, ne pas is to be added, ne......(verb) pas.

Examples :

Je ne suis pas le professeur	***(je n suee pa le profeseur)***
Tu n'as pas Indien.	***(tu naa pa andien)***
Il n'est pas mon ami.	***(eel ne pas maun amee)***
Elle n'est pas très gentil.	***(l ne pas thre jentil)***
Je n'ai pas le stylo.	***(je ne pa le steelo)***

L'exercise :

A. Presently you and your classmate are having some of the objects, write in French the five objects you are possessing.

e.g. J'ai le crayon.	***(je le khroyon)***
J'ai le bouteille d'eau.	***(je le boutille do)***

B. Ecrivez en francais le sentences suivant

1) You don't have the car.
2) She doesn't have the book.
3) He is nnot having the pen.
4) We are having the bottle.

Answers :

B. 1) Tu n'as pas la voiture.	***(tu na pa la vchuyu)***
2) Elle n'a pas le livre.	***(el na pa le leevre)***
3) Il n'pas·le stylo	***(eel na pa le steelo)***
4) Nous n'avons pas le bouteille	***(nooz navo pa le boutille)***

Possessive adjectives

They always come before a noun. Like other adjectives, they agree in gender and number wiith the noun ;the masculine and feminine plural are identical :

Singular	**Plural**	**English**	
Masc	**Fem**		
Mon***(maun)***	ma***(maa)***	mes***(me)***	my
Ton***(tau)***	ta ***(ta)***	tes***(tez)***	your
Son***(sau)***	sa***(saa)***	ses***(sez)***	our
Notre***(nothr)***	notre***(nothr)***	nos***(noz)***	our
Votre***(vothr)***	votre ***(vothr)***	vos ***(voz)***	your
Leur***(ler)***	leur ***(ler)***	les***(lez)***	they

The possessive adjective is repeated before each noun and agrees with it :

Use :

1)The possessive adjectives is repeated before each noun and agrees with it ;

i) **Mon père et ma mère sont avec moi.**
(Maun peha maun meh son avec mua.) My father and my mother are with me.

Here father is masculine therefore mon and mother feminine therefore ma , we are talking of more than one person therefore « sont ».

ii) **Elle a ma voiture.**
(L a maa vachyu.) She is having my car.

Here car is feminine therefore ma.

2) son/sa/ses

They can all mean his, her or its. In French, the form of the adjective is determined by the gender and number of the noun that follows, and not by the possessor.

Il apporte sa château
(Eel apporhte saa shatau) he is bringing his hat.

Here hat is feminine therefore sa is used.

Je utilise mon stylo
(Je utileeze maun steelo) I am using my pen.

Here pen is masculine.

3)ton/ta/tes and votre / vos

The two sets of words for « your », ton/ta/tes and votre/vos, correspond to the two different forms tu and vous ; they must be used together with the same person.

Tu parles á ta mère?
(Tu pakhl a ta meh) Aro you talking to your mother?

Here mother is feminlne.

Est-ce que tu n'a pas ton stylo ?
(esk tu na pa taun steelo) Do you have your pen ?

Here pen is masculine.

Possessive Pronouns

Masculine	Feminine	Plural (masculine/feminine)	
Le mien	la mienne	les mien(ne)s	mine

Le tien	la tienne	les tien(ne)s	yours
Le sien	la sienne	les sien(ne)s	his/her/its
Le nôtre	la nôtre	les nôtres	ours
Le vôtre	la vôtre	les vôtres	yours
Le leur	la leur	les leurs	theirs

Pronunciation in English will remain the same in all the cases :

Mien – ***(meeyen)*** Tien – ***(Teeyen)***

Sien- ***(Seeyen)*** Nôtre – ***(nothr)***

Vôtre –***(vothr)*** Leur – ***(leur)***

Quelle livre il étudies, c 'est le mienne ou le tienne ?
(Kel leevr eel etudeeye, se le meeyen ouu le teeyen.)
Book which he is reading, it is yours or mine.

Êtes vous á votre maison ?
(Eth vooz a vothr maizo.) Are you at your home ?

Á or de + possessive pronoun

The preposition á or de combine with the articles le and les in the usual way :

á+le mien	au mien***(o meeyen)***
á+ les miens	aux miens ***(o meeyen)***
á +les miennes	aux miennes***(o meeyen)***
de+ le mien	du mien ***(doo meeyen)***
de+les miens	des miens***(dez meeyen)***
de +les miennes	des miennes ***(dez meeyen)***

Tu demande tes parents , je demande aux mienne
I*(Tu deeman te paho, je deemand au meeyen.)*
You ask your parents, I ask mine.

Here we have used the term parent initially therefore we are not using the term parent again so use **aux mine**. If we want to use the term parent then the sentence will be :

Tu demande tes parents, je demande mes parents.
You ask your parents, I ask my parents.

L'exercise

A.Deux amis John and Joseph parlent entre deux, traduction en français :

John - My father is an engineer and mother is a housewife.
Joseph – My mother is a professeur . lam the college student.
John - Stephanie is having my camera ?
Joseph – no she is having mine.
John - sorry !

Joseph – no problem ! your brother is a college student or school student?
John - He is a college student and my sister is school student.

B. Traduction les phrases suivant en anglais.

1) Elle est très timide. ***(I a thre teemeed)***
2) Je n'ai pas les timbres. ***(je ne pa lez teembre)***
3) Elle a besoin de la .serviette. ***(I a bezuan the la sehveeyete)***
4) Tu as trop gros. ***(tu a thro grho)***
5) Nous n'avons pas notre livre. ***(nouz na avons paa nothr leevr.)***

Answers :

A.John - Mon père est ingénieur et ma mère est la femme de foyer.
(Maun peh a angeneeyeur a ma meh a la farm de foyer.)
Joseph – Ma mère est professeur. Je suis le lycée.
(Ma meh a professeyueur. Je suee le leece)
John- Stephanie a mon appareil photo ?
(Steephanie a maun apparehel photo.)
Joseph – no, elle a mien.
(No, I a meeyen)
John- pardon ou desolée. Votre père est le lycée ou l'étudiant ?
(Pakhdon ou dezolee. Vothr peh a le leece ou atudeeyent.)
John- Il est lycée et ma sœur est l'étudiante.(sister is feminine)
(L a leece a ma sir a atudeeyent.)

B. 1) She is ver shy
2) I don't have the stamps
3) She needs towel
4) You are very fat
5) We don't have our book.

Lequel

Its literally means « which » , Lequel is a pronoun that replaces the adjective quel and the noun it modifies. It expresses **which one**?
It has four different forms, since it must agree with the noun it refers to:

Gender	**Singular**	**Plural**
Masculine	**lequel*(leekel)***	**lesquels*(lezkel)***
Feminine	**laquelle*(lakel)***	**lesquelles*(lezkel)***

Lequel etc. combines with the prepositions á and de as follows :

A+lequel	auxquel
Á +lesquels	auxquels
Á +lesquelles	auxquelles ?

Okel is the prnonunciation in all the caeses.

De+lequel — duquel ***(dookel)***
De+lesquels — desquels ***(dekel)***
De+lesquelles — desquelles***(dezkel)***

Quel livre veux-tu ? — **Which book do you want?**
(Kel leevr v tu?)

Here we are asking the type of book.

Lequel veux-tu ? [Quel livre ?] Which one do you want?
(Leekel v tu?)

Here we are assking the name of the book among all.

Je veux la pomme lá-bas. — **I want the apple over there.**
(Je v la paume laa bhas.)
Laquelle ? [Quelle pomme ?] — Which one? [Which apple?]
(Laakel)

Je pense á mon frère. — **I'm thinking about my brother.**
(Je paunse a maun fre).
Auquel penses-tu ? [Á quel frère...] Which one are you thinking about?
(Okel paunse tu?)

Le livre dans lequel j'ai écrit...
(Le leevr dans leekel jai achree.) The book in which I wrote...

La ville á laquelle je songe...
(La veel a lakel je saunge). — The town about which I'm dreaming...

Le cinéma **près duquel** j'ai mangé...
(Le cinema phre dookel)

The theater **near which** I ate... **OR** The theater I ate **near**...

Nouns, Articles and Demonstrative Adjectives

All nouns in French have a gender, either masculine or feminine. For the most part, you must memorize the gender, but there are some endings of words that will help you decide which gender a noun is. Nouns ending in –age, ir and –meant are usually masculine, as are nouns ending with a consonant. Nouns ending in –ure, -sion, -ence, -ance, -té, and –ette are usually feminine.

Articles and adjectives must agree in number and gender with the nouns they modify. And articles have to be expressed even though they aren't always in English, and you may have to repeat the article in some cases. Demonstrative are like strong definite articles.

La voiture ***(laa vachyu)***	–	The car
La boutique ***(la bootik)***	–	The butique
Le livre ***(leevr)***	–	The book
La jupe ***(laa jup)***	–	The skirt
La masion ***(la maizo)***	–	The house
La serviette ***(la sehveeyet)***	–	The napkin or the towel
La été ***(la ate)***	–	The summer
La gestion ***(la gausteeyon)***	–	The administration

Definite articles (The)- The French **definite** article corresponds to **the** in English. These article indicates a **specific** noun

Masculine	feminine	Before vowel	Plural
Le lit	la pomme	l'oiseaux	les garcon
(le lee)	***(la paume)***	***lozo***	***(le gakhson)***
Le livre	la boutique	l'hôtel	les femme
(Le leevr)	***(laa booteek)***	***(lotel)***	***(lez farm)***

e.g

Je vais á la banque ***(Je vaiz a la baunk)*** I'm going to the bank

Here you are specifying the place where you are going.

Voici le livre que j'ai lu ***(Vaizi le leevr k jai tu.)*** Here is the book I read.

Here you are specifying the book which you have already read.

Indefinite articles(A, An, Some) - The singular **indefinite** articles in French correspond to **a**, **an**, or **one** in English.

Masculine	**feminine**
Un ami***(yun amee***)	une amie***(yun amee)***
Un livre(***a leevr)***	une fille***(yun fee)***

e.g.

Il y a un étudiant dans la salle

(Eelya un atudeeyaunt) There is one student in the room.

Here you are only generally specifying the student

J'ai une soeur –

(Jai yun sir.) I have one sister.

Here you are specifying the sister in general.

Partitive Articles: The partitive articles in French correspond to **some or any** in English. There are four forms of the French partitive article.

Masculine(de+le)	**feminine**	**Before vowel**	**Plural**
Du	**de la**	**de l'**	**des**
Du pain	de la glace	de l'eau	des bonbons

(Doo paan)	*(de la glass)*	*(de lo)*	*(dez bonbon)*
Du thè	de la bière	de l'huile	des grafitis
(Doo thee)	*(de la bear)*	*(de hui)*	*(dez grafeetee)*

Note : de + la remains unchanged.

Prepositions: They are those little words that are placed in front of nouns in order to indicate a relationship that noun and a verb, an adjective, or another noun.

Je vais **á** Paris – Iam going to Paris
(J vai a pahi).

Tu es **dans** la salle – You are in the room
(Tu a danz la saal.)

Le stylo **est** pour toi – The pen is for you.
(Le steelo a pur tua.)

Forms with the Prepositions "a" and "de"

1) with á (to,at)
   - á+le = au
   - á+les = aux
   - á+la = do not change

au restaurant***(o resthoro)***, au banque***(o bonc)***, aux enfants***(o onfo)***.

2) with de(of, from)
   - De+le = du
   - De +les = des
   - De +la = do not change

De la région***(de l regeo)*** , des chômeurs ***(des chomer)***, du directeur ***(du directer)***.

More prepositions are depuis, á côté de, dans, en, avec,contre,en, durant,entre,par, parmien face de, sans sûr, vers

Depuis deux ans je reste ici. Since two years I am staying here.
(Depui d o je resth ici.)

Elle est avec son frère. She is with her brother.
(L a avec saun freh.)

Ma masion est á côté de la banque. My home is **nest** to the bank.
(Maa maizo a a cote de la baunk.)

Je vais vers deux heures. I am **going around** 2'o clock.
(Je vais veh dez a.)

Le Leçon 4

Questions and answers

In French when you are agreed on something it is replied by **"Oui"** which means **Yes** in English and if you are not agreed then it is replied by **"Non"** which means **No** in English.

How the sentences are framed while asking questions.e.g you want to ask the profession of the person that is he advocate.

1) Vous êtes le avocate?
   (Voo zet le avocaat.)
2) Est ce-que vous êtes le avocate?
   (Esk voos zet le avocaat.)
3) Quest ce que vous êtes le avocate?
   (Kesk voos zet le avocaat.)

1) If you want to give answer simply in Yes or No, then form the question by using est-

Est- ce que?

a) Est-ce-que tu anglais? – Oui.
   (eskk tu onglaee.)(ouee)
b) Est-ce-que Vous êtes l'avocate? – Non
   (Esk vooz zet lavocat) – No
c) Est-ce-que tu vas au banque? – Yes
   (Esk tu va o bonc) (Ouee)

2) You can also form a yes-no question simply by keeping the same words as in the equivalent affirmative sentence but by saying the final syllable on a rising pitch:

a) tu as anglais? – Oui, je suis anglais.
   (tu a onglee) ***(ouec, je suee onglee)***
b) Vous êtes l'avocate? – Non, je suis l'architect
   (vooz zet lavocate) ***(non, je suee lashee tect)***

c) tu vas au banque? – Oui, je vais au banque.
(tu va o bonc) *(ouee, je vae o banc)*

3) The construction qu'est-ce que is also a very common way of asking what... questions but the only differnce here we want to know th answer more than yes or no .

qu'est-ce que tu fais? What are you doing?
Je fais le ménange. I am doing the household work.
(K se k tu fai.)

Here we don't know what the other person is doing.

If we want to know is he doing the household work then the question will be either .

Est-ce que tu fais le ménage?
(Esk tu fai le menaag.)

Tu fais le ménage?
(Tu fai le menaag.)

Framing the questions by using ne pas

One of the easiest ways to ask a question that may be answered by yes/no is to raise the pitch of your voice at the end of a statement. In a declarative statement, the pitch normally falls, to make the sentence negative simply add ne before est ce and pas after ce, **n'est ce pas and que will get removed.**

N'est ce pas tu vas au banque?
(Nes pa tu o baunk.)

N'est ce pas vous prenez?
(Nes pa voos praune.)

Negative Pronouns

Negative pronouns negate, refuse, or cast doubt on the existence of the noun that they replace.

Je n'ai vendu aucun des livres. I haven't sold any of the books.
(Je ne vaundu okyun dez leevr.)

To make a sentence or question negative, place **ne** in front of the conjugated verb and **pas** after it. **Ne...pas** translates roughly as **not**.

Je suis riche - Je ne suis pas riche. I'm rich - I'm not rich.
(Je sueereesh- je n suee pas reesh)

Êtes-vous fatigué? - N'êtes-vous pas fatigué? Are you tired? - Aren't you tired?

(Eth voos fatigue – neth voos pas fatigue.)

With compound verbs and dual-verb constructions, the negative adverbs surround the conjugated verb.*

Je n'ai pas étudié. ***(Je ne suee pas atudeeye.)***	I didn't study.
Nous n'aurions pas su. ***(Noos naurion pas su.)***	We wouldn't have known.
Il ne sera pas arrive. ***(El ne sehra pas arheeve.)***	He won't have arrived.
Tu n'avais pas parlé ? ***(Tu nave pas pakhle.)***	You hadn't talked?
Il ne veut pas skier. ***(El n v paa skeeye.)***	He doesn't want to ski.
Je ne peux pas y aller. ***(Je ne p pas y allee.)***	I can't go.

*Except for *nulle part*, which follows the main verb.

When there is an indefinite article or partitive article in a negative construction, it changes to **de**, meaning **any**.

> J'ai une pomme ==> Je n'ai pas de pomme.
> ***(jai eyun paume0 (je ne pas de paume)***
> I have an apple ==> I don't have any apples.

In informal and familiar spoken French, *ne* is often dropped.

> Je ne sais pas > Je sais pas.
> ***(je ne say pa) (je say pa)***
> I don't know.

Related negative adverbs

ne...pas encore - *(ne pa oncore)* not yet

Il n'est pas encore arrivé

(eel ne pa oncor arrive) He has not arrived yet.

ne...pas toujours - *(ne pa tuju)* not always

Je ne mange pas toujours ici

(je ne maung pa tuju ecee) I don't always eat here

ne...pas du tout - ***(ne pa duu tuu)*** **not at all**
Je n'aime pas du tout les épinards
(je name pas du tut lez apnard) I don't like spinach at all.

ne...nullement –(na nelmo)not at all
Il ne veut nullement venir
(eel ne v nulmo veneer) He doesn't want to come at all.

ne...nulle part (na nulpa) - nowhere
Je ne l'ai trouvé nulle part
(je ne lat throuve nel pah) I couldn't find it anywhere.

ne...aucunement (na ocunmo)- not at all
Je ne te manque aucunement?
(je ne te monk ocunmo) You don't miss me at all?

ne...plus (na plus)- no more, not anymore
Vous n'y travaillez plus
(vooz nee thavaye plus) You don't work there anymore.

ne...jamais (na jame)- never
Nous ne voyageons jamais
(nooz ne voyageo jamai) We never travel.

ne...guère (na gueh)- hardly, barely, scarcely
Il n'y a guère de monde
(eel nee ya geh de maund) There's hardly anyone there.

Il n'a rien fait.*(eel na rhian)* He hasn't done anything or He's done nothing.

Je ne connais personne ici.
(je ne coone pehson ecee) I don't know anyone here.

The French **negative pronouns** are:

ne... aucun(e) **(de)****(ocun)***	none (of), not any (of)
ne... nul(le) ***(nul)***	no one
ne... pas un(e) **(de)*** ***(pa eun)***	not one (of)
ne... pas un(e) **seul**(e) **(de)***	not a single one (of)
ne... personne ***(ne pehson)***	no one
ne... quiconque*(ne queecon)*	no one
Ne... rien*(ne rhian)*	nothing, not...anything

Negative pronouns can be the **subject**, **direct object**, or ***indirect object*** of a sentence.

Personne ne m'a vu.	***(pehson ne ma voo)***	No one saw me.
Je ne vois personne.	***(je ne vua pehson)***	I don't see anyone.

Je ne pense á *personne.* ***(je ne paunse pehson)*** I'm not thinking about *anyone*.

*These pronouns must always have an antecedent. In addition, because they express a quantity, en must be used when these pronouns are the direct object of the sentence.

Aucun de mes amis n'est venu.
(Ocun de mez amee ne venu) None of my friends came.
Mes amis ? Aucun n'est venu.
(mez amee?ocun ne venu) My friends? None came.
Mes amis ? Je n'en ai vu aucun.
(Mez amee?Je no a vu ocoon) My friends? I didn't see any of them.

With compound verbs and dual-verb constructions, negative pronouns surround the conjugated verb.*
Je n'ai rien fait.
(Je nc rhian fe) I didn't do anything.
Je n'ai pas vu un de mes amis.
(Je ne pas vyu a de mez amee) I didn't see one of my friends.

*Except for *personne* and *aucun*, which follow the main verb.

The negative conjunction **ne... ni... ni** (neither... nor) is used in exactly the same way as negative pronouns, with **ne** preceding the verb and each **ni** preceding one of the negated qualities, people, etc.
Tu n'es ni sympa ni charmant.
(tyu ne nee sympaa nee chamo) You are neither nice nor charming.
Ni Pierre ni Marie ne sont venus.
(nee peeh nee mare ne so venu) Neither Pierre nor Marie came.

L'exercise

A.Récrirez les sentences par utilisez est -ce-que ou n'est ce pas-

(a) Tu aimes regarder le television (est-ce que)
(tu aim regardeh le televizio)
(b) Vous venez dans ma maison (n'est ce pas)
(***vooz vene danz ma maiso)***
(c) Elle est intéressée pour le film (est-ce-qu)
(el a anthereso pur le film)
(d) Vous mangez le petit dejeuner sans moi(est-ce-que)
(vooz mange le petit dejeuneh sau mua)
(e) Elle aime lire (n'est ce pas)
(el aim leeh)

(f) Tex et Tommy voyagent ensemble(est-ce-que)
(tex a tommy voyajo osaumble)

B. Changez les phrases suivant en français:

(a) I can't see anyone in the cafeteria.
(b) My none of the friends have come to meet me
(c) I will never eat chocolates.
(d) I don't eat carrots at all.
(e) I hardly get time to watch television.
(f) Will you never maary at all?
(g) I will hardly ask you to help me.
(h) I never buy grocery on Sunday.
(i) Nothing can change my decision.
(j) I can't nowhere find my shoes.

Answers :

A.. a Est-ce que tu aimes regarder le t élévision?
(Esk tu aim regardhe le televizio)
b N'est ce pas vous venez dans ma maison?
(Nes pa vooz vene danz ma maizo)
c Est-ce que elle est intéressée pour le film?
(Esk el a anthresse pur le film)
d Est-ce que vous mangez le petit dejeuner sans moi?
(Esk vooz mange le petit dejene sau mua)
e N'est ce pas elle aime lire?
(Nes pa el aim leeh)
f. Est-ce que Tex et Tommey voyagent ensemble?
(Esk Tex a Tommt voyajo onsaumble)

B. a. Je ne vois aucun dans le cafeteria.
(je ne vua ocun danz le cafeterea)
b. Aucun de mes amis ne rien.
(ocun de mez amee ne rhia)
c. Je ne mange jamais le chocolates.
(je ne maunj jamai le shokokala)
d. Je ne mange pas du tout. les carrots.
(je ne maunj pa du tut lez cahot)
e. Je n'ai guére de temps en regarder le television.
(je nai gueh de taump o regardeh le tele vizio)

f. Tu ne maries pas du tout.
(tu ne mahee pa du tut)

g. Je ne demande guére de m'aider
(je ne deemand gueh de maide)

h. Je n'achete jamais provision en dimanche.
(je nasheet jamai prhovizio o deemaksh)

i. Rien change ma decision.
(Rhia chang ma decizio)

j. Je ne trouve nullement mes chausseurs.
(je ne throiv nulmo mez shauser)

Le Leçon 5

Countries

As explained every object has a gender, in the same way countries also have a gender.

En, au, aux, á before the names of a country, city or geographical place. Feminine are those countries which either starting with vowel or ending with vowel.

Country :	**To or in**	**From**
Masculine	au	du
Feminine	en	de / d'
Plural	aux	des

La France(f)	*(la fonce)*
L'Italie(f)	*(leetalie)*
La Belgique,(m)	*(la belgeek)*
aux États-Unis (p)	*(o etazuni)*
L'Allemagne (f)	*(laamaigne)*
Le Mexique (m)	*(le mexick)*
Le Canada (m)	*(le Canada)*
L'Australie (f)	*(laustralee)*
La Russie (f)	*(la rucee)*
L'Espagne(f)	*(lespaine)*
Le Japon(m)	*(le jàpo)*
La Suisse(f)	*(le suis)*
La Hollande (f)	*(laholand)*
L'Inde(f)	*(l aand)*
L'Afrique(f)	*(l afreek)*
La Chine(f)	*(l cheen)*

We have learnt the gender of the countries, continents too have theior gender, they are always masculine.

Nationalities:

Nationality is translated as "Nationalité" in French and the gender is female, if we are referring to the nationality of the female then add (e) at the end Let us take the above countries to know the nationalities.

Country	Nationalities
La France(f)	français(e) *(francaiz)*
L'Italie(f)	Italién (ne) *(eetalia)*
La Belgique,(m)	Belge *(belj)*
aux États-Unis (p)	Américain(e) *(american)*
L'Allemagne (f)	Allemande(e) *(almand)*
Le Mexique (m)	Mexicain(E) *(mexeecan)*
Le Canada (m)	Canadien(ne) *(canedian)*
L'Australie (f)	australien(ne) *(ostralia)*
La Russie (f)	Russe *(rooz)*
L'Espagne(f)	Espagnol(e) *(aspaneol)*
Le Japon(m)	Japonais(e) *(japonai)*
La Suisse(f)	Suisse *(suisee)*
La Hollande (f)	Hollandais(e) *(holandae)*
L'Inde(f)	Indien(ne) *(andean)*
L'Afrique(f)	Africain(e) *(afreecan)*
La Chine(f)	Chinois(e) *(sheenoi)*

Le Leçon 6

Verbs: A verb is the action word in a sentence. It is the word that says what happens, discusses an action, or describes a state of being. French verbs must be conjugated (inflected).

There are three main conjugations in french which are determined by infinitive endings. The first conjugation ending with **–er,** and will be referred to as **–er** verbs, the second conjugation verbs ending with **-ir** and will be referred to as **–I, the third conjugation verbs ending with –re** and and will be referred to as **–re** verbs **r** verbs The blanks in these sentences can only be filled with verbs.

I _____ tired (am, feel, look)
He ____ to the store (went, walks)
We _____ books (hate, collect, read)

Let us learn some of the common verbs and their conjugations which can be used very frequently.

Être(to be)	Avoir(to have)	Finir(to finish)
Je suis***(je suee)***	J'ai***(zai)***	Je finis***(j finee)***
Tu es ***(tu aa)***	Tu as ***(tu aa)***	Tu finis***(tu finee)***
Il/Elle est***(eel a)***	Il/Elle a***(eel a)***	Il/Elle finit***(eel finee)***
Nous sommes ***(noo zom)***	Nous avons ***(noo zavo)***	Nous finissions ***(noo fineeso)***.
Vous êtes***(voo zet)***	Vous avez***(voo zave)***	Vous finissez***(voo feenise)***
Ils/Elles sont***(eel zo)***	Ils/Elles ont***(eel zo)***	Ils/Elles finissent***(eel feeniso)***

Aller(to go).	Venir(to come)	Demander(to ask)
Je vais***(je ve)***	Je viens***(je veeya)***	Je demande***(je demand)***
Tu vas***(tu va)***	Tu viens ***(tu veeya)***	Tu demandes***(tu demand)***
Il/Elle va***(eel va)***	Il/Elle Vient ***(el veeya)***	Il/Elle demande***(el demand)***

Vous allez *(vvoz zale)*	Vous venez *(vooz vene)*	Vous demandez *(vooz deemande)*
Nous allons *(noo zalo)*	Nous venons *(noo veno)*	Nous demandons *(noo deemando)*
Ils/Elles vont *(eel vo)*	Ils/Elles viennent *(eel veeyen)*	Ils/Elles demandent *(eel demand)*

Appeler means to call but while introducing someone or yourself verb s'appeller is used:

Appeler

J'appelle *(japel)*
Tu appelles *(tu appel)*
Il/Elle appelle *(el appel)*
Nous appelons *(nooz apelo)*
Vous appelez *(vooz appele)*
Ils/Elles appellent *(eel appele)*

S'appeler

Je s'appelle *(je sapael)*
Tu s' appelles *(tu sapel)*
Il/Elle s'appelle *(eel sapel)*
J'habite á Paris *(jabeet a pahee)*
Tu fais le gateâu *(tu feh le gato)*
Il s'appelle Sophie *(eel sapel sofee)*
Elle demande pour le thè. *(el deemand pur le the)*
Vous allez au banque. *(voozale o bonc)*
Je vois le film *(je vua le film)*
Nous finissons le travallle *(nooz feeneeso le thavayee)*
Elle demande dc Bernard *(el deemand de behnahd)*
Vous voulez le congé *(vooz voole le conje)*

Qui êtes-vous ?

Please find below the dialogue which is taking between two people which will relect on the basic greetings and the general communication to introduce yourself.

-Bonjour madam ! *(bonju madam)*
-Bonjour monsieur ? *(bonju meseur)*

-Je m'appelle Peter et vous	***(je mapel peter a voo)***
-Je m'appelle Stephanie ?	***(je mapel stefanee)***
-Madam,est ce que Vous êtes Français?	***(madam, esk vooz zet fonsaiz)***
-Non, Je suis espagnole et vous ?	***(non, je suee aspaneol a voo)***
- Je suis anglais.	***(je suee ongle)***
- qu'est ce que vous faites ?	***(Kesk voo fait)***
- Je suis l'avoact, au revoir Peter.	***(je suee lavocat, avwah peter)***
- Au revoir Stephanie.	***(avwah steefanee)***

By reading the above definition of verbs, formation of the verbs will not become easy. There is a key point to remember and form the conjugation of the verb.

Verbs ending in –cer

Verbs ending in **–cer** require a cedilla under the **c(ç)** before an **a** or an **o to preserve the soft sound of the** c:

Commencer

Je commence	***(je kmonse)***
Tu commences	***(je kmonse)***
Il/Elle commence	***(eel kmonse)***
Nous commençons	***(nooz kmonso)***
Vous commencez	***(vooz kmonsez)***
Ils/Elles commencent	***(el kamonso)***

Verbs ending in –ger

Verbs ending in **–ger** require an **–e** after the **g** before an a or an **o** to preserve the soft sound of the g **:**

Manger

Je mange	***(je maunj)***
Tu manges	(***tyu maunj)***
Il/Elle mange	***(eel maunj)***
Nous mangeons	***(noo mangeo)***
Vous mangez	***(voo manzez)***
Ils/Elles mangent	***(eel manzo)***

L'exercise

You are meeting your friend after an year, write conversation.

Le Leçon 7

La description de le parc

Il ya beaucoup des persons dans le parc, la madam est Allemagne et l'homme est l'Américan. Vous voyez que les enfants jouer.
L'Allemagne est seul, Il ya deux plus personnes qui parler. Il ya un bassin dans le parc mais pas fleurs.

(eelya bucou dez pehson danz le park, la madaam a almaigne a lome a lamerican. Vooz voyez k lezonfo joue. Laagmne a sel, eelya deux pluz pehsonne kee parkhl. Eelya un basseen danz le park meh pa fler)

La description de ma famille

C'est ma famille.Il ya quatre personne. Mon père ,Il s'appelle John et il est l'avocat. Ma mere Stephanie, elle est femme au foyer. Mon frère Peter, il est i'etudiant et moi je m'appelle Lynnet, je suis l'etudiant du lycée technique.Nous habitons près de le banque RBI. J'aime ma famille le beaucop.

(se ma famel. Elya cath pehson. Maun peh eel sapel John a eel a lavocat.
Ma meh Stephanie, el a farm au foyeh. Maun freh Peter, eel a letudiant a mua jamepel Leenet, je suee letudiant du lycee technick. Nouz abiton preh de baunk RBI. Jem ma fameel le bucou.)

Exercsie 1

Deux amis recontrent après longtemp, écrivez les conversation.

Exercise 2

Les formes de politesse

Christian present son ami Louis au Parents, il ya les conversation.

Christian : Papa, rendez vous mon ami Louis.
(papa, rendez vooz maun amee luis)
MonsieurJoffre : Ah, Bonjour, Louis. Comment cava?
(ah, bonju, luis. Commo sava)
Louis: Je suis trés bien et vous ?
(je suee thre bean a vooz)
Madam Joffre: Çava bien.
(sava bean)
Monsieur : Vous êtes américain, je crois?
(voozet amereecan, je khua)
Louis: Non, Je suis africain.
(je suee afreecan)

Formation du plural

In French nouns are always either singular or plural. It is usually introduced by the determiner, which reflects the number of the noun.
As in English, the plural is formed by adding an – **s** to the singular form of the noun.

1) in the same way there are most of the noun form their plural by adding **s** to the singular:

Le vin*(le vin)* le vins*(le vin)*
Un étudiante*(un atudeeant)* des étudiants*(un atudeeant)*

2) Nouns ending **in s,x, or z** remain unchanged:

le bras ***(le bha)***	**les bras*(le bha)***
la voix ***(le vua)***	**les voix** ***(le vua)***
le nez ***(le nez)***	**les nez*(le nez)***

3) Nouns ending in **–au, -eau and** eu add **x** to the singular:

Le tuyaux ***(tu tuyo)***	**les tuyaux*(tu tuyo)***
Le bateau (***le bato)***	**les bateaux*(le bato)***
Le jeu ***(le jo)***	**les jeux** ***(le jo)***

4) Nouns ending in **–al** change to **–aux;**

le journal(*le journal)*	**les journaux*(lez journo)***

5) Nouns ending in **–ail** change to **–aux**

le bail ***(le bai)***	**les baux*(lez ba)***
le travail (***le thavai)***	**les travaux*(lez thravo)***

6)Nouns ending in –ou:

a)Seven nouns ending in in-**ou** add **x** in the plural:

le bijou ***(le beeju)***	**les bijoux*(lez bijuu)***
le caillou ***(le caillo)***	**les cailloux(*lex caillo*)**
le chou ***(le shu)***	**les choux*(lez shu)***
le geneou*(le geno)*	**les genoux(*lez geno)***
le hibou ***(le eebo)***	**les hiboux*(le eebo)***
le jQujou(*le jujo)*	**les joujoux(*lez jujo)***
le pou(*le po)*	**les poux*(le po)***

b) There are some of the nouns which are ending in **–ou** add s to make them plural;

le clou(*le clu)*	**les clous*(le clu)***

7) Irregular nouns

un œil*(un oee)*	**des yeux** ***(dez eex)***
le ciel ***(le ciel)***	**les cieux** ***(lex cieu)***
Monsieur*(maunseur)*	**Messieurs*(masseur)***
Mademoiselle*(madamozel)*	**Mesdemoiselles*(mezdumoizel)***
Madame*(madam)*	**Mesdames*(mezdam)***

Le Leçon 8

What is a pronoun?

A pronoun is a word used in place of one or more nouns, and finding the right pronoun in French depends mainly on knowing exactly what you are going to replace. So the first thing is to be able to recognize the objects in your sentences; objects being nouns that indicate towards whom or what the action of the verb is directed. To make it a little easier, we are going to divide the objects into only two main categories : the direct object or the indirect object.

The direct object is the complement, which indicates the object of the action expressed by the verb.

The indirect object also indicates the object of the action expressed by the verb, but it's structure is different; the complement is linked to the verb by a preposition.
(In French : á, de, pour, avec, contre...)

1) Forms

PERSON	Direct object	Indirect object
Je	me(m')	moi
Tu	te(t')	toi
Il/ elle	le(l'), la(l')	lui
Nous	nous	nous
Vous	vous	vous
Ils/Elles	les	leur

Note:me,te,le and la changes to m', t', and l' before vowel or silent h.

En replaces expression of quantity, un, une, des, du, de la, de l', idea thing.

- Je bois trop de vin — ***(je bua thro de vin)***
  Je bois en vin — ***(je bua e va)***

-Je parle á John	***(je pakhl a john)***
Je lui parle	***(je luee pakhl)***
-J'ai le deux stylo	***(jai le deux steelo)***
J'ai le deux	***(jai le deux)***
-Tu recontre Stephanie	***(tu reconthr Stephanie)***
Tu la recontre	***(tu la reconthr)***
-Tu vas avec Bernard	***(tu vas avec behnard)***
Tu lui vas	***(tu luee va)***

2) In French, object pronouns come immediately before the verb they refer to. With a compound tense, they come before the auxiliary:

Nous t'attendons ici

(nous taando ici) we will wait for you here

Je lui parle du examen prochain

(je luee pakhl du exama proshain) I am talking to her about the next exam

Vous leur attendez ici

(vooz ler attinde ici) are you waiting for them here

3) Indirect object pronouns replace a noun that follows the verb with a linking preposition (usually á+"to"). They answer the question to "who(m)?"

Á qui tu parles?-

Je Parle á Marc***(Je pakhl a Marc)***
Je lui parle ***(je luee pakhl)*** (replacing by noun)

Avec qui Vous allez au fête?

Nous allons avec madam " Lusi"
(nouzalo avex madam Lusi)
Nous lui allonc ***(nooz luee allo)***

Demonstrative pronouns (this one, that one, the one[s], these, those) refer to a **previously-mentioned noun** in a sentence. They must agree with the gender and number of the noun(s).

	singular	**plural**
masculine	**celui(*celuee*)**	**ceux(s)**
feminine	**celle(*sel*)**	**celles(*sel*)**

Each of the four **demonstrative pronouns** can refer to something nearby or far away (e.g., **celui** can mean this one or that one).

Demonstrative pronouns cannot stand alone; they must be used in one of the following constructions:
1) either with ci or lá, you can distinguish between **this one** and **that one**, **these** and **those** with the suffixes **-ci** (here) and **-lá** (there).

Quelle fille l'a fait, celle-ci ou celle-lá ?
(kel fee la feh, sel see ou sel ca)
Which girl did it, this one or that one?

Je ne sais pas si je veux ceux-ci ou ceux-lá.
(je ne se pa see je ve s see ou s la)
I don't know if I want this one or that one.

2) usually introduced by de to indicate possession or origin

Quel film veux-tu voir ? Celui de la France ou celui du Canada ?
(kel feelm ve tu vua? Celuee de la fonce ou celuee du Canada)
Which film do you want to see? The one from France or (the one from) Canada?

3) Followed by a relative pronoun + dependent clause

Celui qui a menti sera puni.
(celuee kee a maunti sera puni) He who / Whoever lied will be punished.

Ceux qui sont polis reçevront un cadeau.
(se kee so pole recevro un cado) Those who are polite will receive a gift.

Le Leçon 9

How to replace a noun that refers to a place by "En" or "Y"?

There is another category that is important but doesn't fit in the preceding table because it's neither a direct object nor an indirect object : it's the nouns that refer to place or location. Whenever you want to replace a location by a pronoun, you have to check what the preposition Is.

- If the preposition is "de" (or a contraction of it), the pronoun is going to be EN.As explained in the last chapter it replaces "expression of quantity, un, une, des, du, de la, de l', idea thing."
- If the preposition is anything else (á, chez, dans, etc..., anything that indicates a location), the pronoun is going to be Y.

"EN"

En is used instead of de + noun. Since **de** has a variety of meaning, **en** can be used in a number of ways:

It means "of it/them", but also "with it/them", "about it/them", "from it / there", "out of it/there"

tu es sûr du prix?-j'en suis sûr
(tu as sur du preex- jau suee suh)

Nous pensons de la fête – Nous en pensons
(noos paunso de la fete- nouzo paunso)

Elle est folle des animaux – elle en est folle
(el a fol dez aneemo-el on a fol))

Il revient de Belgique- il en revient.
(eel revia de belgeek- eel o reveean)

Je te remercie de ta carte- Je t'en remericc
(je te remchcoo de ta cakht – je taun rehmercee)

Vous avez besoin de ces papiers- Vous en avez besoin.
(voozave bezuan de ces pahpeear- vooz an avez besuan)

"Y"

Y is used instead of á+noun(not referring to a person). It is used:

1) As the indirect object of a verb. Since the preposition á is translated in a variety of ways in English, y may have various (it, of it/them, about it / them. Etc.)

Tu joues au bridge?-j'y joues rarement
(Tu ju o breedge ?- jee ju rehmo)

Vous venez de Páris?- Oui, Nous y venont
(vooz vene de pahee ?- ouee, nouzee veno)

Il regard á la fontaine- Non, Il y regard
(eel regard a la faunten- Non, eel e reagrdh)

2) It must always be used with the verb **aller - to go** when the place is not mentioned in the clause. It is often not translated in English:

Comment vas-tu á l'école?-j'y vais en bus.
(Cammo va tu a lecol?-jee vae a bus)

Allons-y! Nous y venons demain
(allozee ! nouzee veno dema)

N'y allez pas !
(nee alle pa)

L'exercise

Rempliez des blancs pay en ou y.

1) elle est chez le medicin. ***(el a shez le medeesa)***	elle .....est.
2) veux –tu du thé? ***(v tu de the)***	...veux-tu?
3) Je vais . ***(je vay)***	Je....vais.
4) Je vais chez moi ***(je vay chez mua)***	J'.....vais.
5) Nous cherchons un appartement. ***(nooz shersho un apakhtmo)***	Nous....cherchons un appartement.

6) Vous avez trop de problems. ***(voozave thro de peohblem)***	Vous ... Avez trop.
7) Nous avons beaucoup de jouets ***(nooz zavo bucou de joue)***	Nous en avons beaucoup.

Answers:

A.1) Elle y est.	***(el e a)***
2) en veux tu?	***(a v tu)***
3) J'y vais.	***(jee vay)***
4) J en vais.	***(jau vay***
5) Nous en cherchons un appartment	***(nooz o shersho a apkhtmo)***
6) Vous en avez trop.	***(voozo avay thro)***
7) Nous en avons beaucoup.	***(nooz o avo bucou)***

Le Leçon 10

Comment, Quand, Où et Quelle.

You have learnt that questions can be asked by using est-ce-que, qu'est-ce que, besides these following can also used to ask questions.

Comment, Quand, Où et Quelle

Comment means How, Pourquoi means why does, Quand means when , où means where and Quelle means what in English.

Quel(masculine)***(kel)***
Quelle(feminine))***(kel)***
Quels(plural))***(kel)***

Comment

1) Immediately after comment verb takes place and then the person:

Comment viens tu ici***?***

(camo veean tu ici) How do you come here

Comment vas tu ?

(camo va tu) How are you

2) If we are using with être, meaning of the comment changes to "what is ....like"

Comment est-il? ***(camo a teel)***

3) Comment is also used to ask someone's name?

Comment t'appelle tu ***?(camo tapel tu)***
Comment s'appelle elle?(***camo sapel el)***

4) Comment is also used if you haven't heard anything or you can't believe.

Sa père mort ! ***(sa peh moth)***

Comment !(***kamo)***

Je n'aime aller avec toi.***(je name alle avez tua)***

Comment!***(kamo)***

Quand – When

Quand vas tu au école? ***(kau va tu a acol)***

Où – Where , it refer to the place

Où allons nous?***(ou allo nooz)***

Quelle

Forms(which, what) agrees in number and gender with the noun it refers to. It has four forms:

-	**Wisth a masculine singular noun**	**quel?**
-	**With a feminine singular noun**	**quelle?**
-	**With a masculine plural noun**	**quels?**
-	**With a feminine plural noun**	**quelles**

I. Quel can be used in simply asking the questions

Quel livre veux-tu ?

(kel leevr ve tu) Which book do you want?

Quel livre est-ce que tu veux ?

(kel leevr a tu ve) What book do you want?

Quelle heure est-il ?

(kel a teel) What time is it?

II. Qucl can be used after a **preposition**

Á quelle heure veux-tu partir ?

(a kel h ve tu pakhteer) What time do you want to leave?

De quels livres est-ce qu'il parle?

(de kel levr a cekeel pakhl) What books is he talking about?

III. Quel can stand alone, followed by **être**

Quel est le problème ?

(kel a le problem) What's the problem?

Quelle est la différence ?

(kel a la deefehronce) What's the difference?

Note: Quel can also be used as an **exclamative adjective**:

Quel bateau !

(kel bato) What a boat!

Quelle catastrophe ! ***(kel cathostrof)***
What a catastrophe

Qui – Who, whom, it is used to refer to people, it can be both subject and object, and can be used after a preposition;

Qui tu vas ?

(kee tu va) With whom yo are going

Qui appele tu ?

t(kee apael tu) whom you are calling

Tu y vas avec qui?

(tu e va avez kee) You are going there with whom?

Que- What, it is used to refer to things, it is only used in direct questions; it is always a direct object and cannot be used after prepositions.

Gender of the Quelle is determined by the object we are talking about.

Que désirez vous? ***(k dezeereh voo)***
Que penses tu? ***(k paunse tu)***
Que veut elle? ***(k v el)***

Note: Que become qu' before a vowel or a silent h.

Quoi- What, it refer to things; it is used instead of que or qu'-est que after a preposition:

Tu pense de quoi? ***(tu paunse de kua)***

Vous parlez avec John de quoi? ***(voo pakhl avec John de kua)***

N'importe comment	***(nampokht camo)***	Any way
N'importe lequel	***(nampokht leekel)***	Any (one)
N'importe où	***(nampokht ou)***	Anywhere
N'importe quand	***(nampokht kaun)***	Anytime

N'importe quel	***(nampokht kel)***	Anything
N'importe qui	***(nampokht kee)***	Anyone
N'importe quoi	***(nampokht kua)***	Anything

L'exercise

A. Faites les questionsdes suivants.

1. Are you (tu) studying French?
2. How many cats do they (male) have?
3. Where does he live?
4. What restaurants do they (female) like?
5. Do we like to travel?
6. Which house are you (vous) buying?
7. Who works in Paris?

Answers :

A.1) Est-ce que tu étidies le français ?
(esk tu atudeeye le foncaiz)

2) Comment de chats est ce que ils ont ?
(kamo de shat esk eelzo)

3) Où habit-t-Il ?
(ou abit til)

4) Quels restaurants aiment elles?
(kel resthoro aime el)

5) Est-ce que nous aimons voyager?
(esk nooz aimo voyajo)

6) Quelle maison achetez vous ?
(kel maizo achete voo)

7) Qui travaile á Paris ?
(kee thavayee a pahee)

Le Leçon 11

Adjectives

Adjectives are describing words that usually accompany a noun(or a pronoun) and tell us what someone or something is like:

Une grande ville ***(eeyun ghand ceel)***	a large city
Un passé-temps intéressant ***(un pas taum antehresoh)***	an interesting hobby
Elle est espagnole (***el a espanol)***	She is Spanish
C'etait ennuyeux ***(seteh annuyox)***	it was boring

Agreement of Adjectives

In French, adjectives agree in number and gender with the noun or pronoun they refer to: This means that, unlike English adjectives, which don';t change, French adjectives have four different forms that are determined by the noun they go with:

-masculine singular for masculine singular words
-feminine singular for feminine singular words
-masculine plural for masculine plural words.
- feminine plural for feminine plural words.

Un passport vert ***(un passpoht veh)***	a green passport
Une voiture verte ***(eun vachyu veh)***	a green car

Des grants verts ***(dez ghant veh)***	green gloves
Des chaussettes vertes (***dez shocet veh)***	green socks

Note : If two singular words share the same adjective, the adjective will be in the plural:

Un foulard et un chapeau rouges ***(un foulahd a un shapo ruze)***	a red scarf and a red hat.

If one of these words is feminine, one masculine, the adjective will be masculine plural:

Une robe et un manteau noirs ***(eun rohb a u nuar)***	a black dress and a black coat

Feminine forms of adjectives

General rule

Add the letter e to the masculine singular form:

Masculine		**Feminine**
Grand	***(ghond)***	Grande ***(ghond)***
Amusant	***(amyuzo)***	Amusante ***(amyuzo)***
Américain	***(amereecan)***	Américaine***(amereecan)***
Un livre amusant	***(un leevr amyuzo)***	la musique amusante ***(la myuzik amyuzo)***

Adjectives already ending in "e"

These do not change:

Masculine	**Feminine**
Rouige***(rooj)***	Rouige ***(rooj)***
Jeune ***(jun)***	Jeune ***(jun)***
Malade ***(malaad)***	Malade ***(malaad)***

Others

The spelling of some adjectives changes when the e is added

The following masculine endings generally double the final consonant before adding e:

Masculine ending	**Feminine Ending**
-el	**-elle**
-eil	**-eille**
-en	**-enne**
-on	**-onne**
-et	**-ette**

examples

Masculine	**Feminine**
Réel***(reel)***	Réelle***(reel)***
Cruel***(khuel)***	Cruelle***(khuel)***
Bas ***(ba)***	Basse***(bas)***
Muet ***(muet)***	Muette***(mut)***
Net ***(net)***	Nette***(net)***

Feminine ending of some common adjectives in **-et** is **-ète** instead of –ette

Masculine	**Feminine**
Complet***(kaumplet)***	complete***(kaumplet)***
Inquiet ***(ankeeyet)***	Inquiète ***(ankeeyet)***
Secret ***(seekhret)***	Secrète ***(seekhret)***

Masculine : ending in **er**, feminine becomes by adding **ère** at the end:

Masculine	**Feminine**
Cher ***(sheh)***	Chère ***(sheh)***
Fier ***(feeyer)***	Fière ***(feeyer)***
Dernier ***(dehneeyer)***	Dernière ***(dehneeyer***

Masculine ending in **x and eur,** feminine becomes by adding **se** in place of x and euse in place of eur:

Masculine	**Feminine**
Heureux***(ah)***	Heureuse***(ahaz)***
Malheureux ***(malahz)***	Malheureuse***(malahz)***

Jaloux ***(jalooz)***	Jalouse ***(jalooz)***
Menteur ***(monter)***	Menteuse***(mauntez)***

But:	doux (**doos**)	douce ***(doos)***
	Faux ***(fau)***	fausse ***(faus)***
	Roux ***(roos)***	rousse***(roos)***
	Vieux ***(vayee)***	vielle ***(veeyel)***

Masculine in **f**, changes to ve to become feminine

Masculine	**feminine**
Neuf ***(nuf)***	Neuve ***(nuv)***
Passif***(pasif)***	Passive ***(passif)***
Positif ***(poseeteev)***	Positive ***(poseeteev)***

Plural of Adjectives:

The masculine and feminine plural of adjectives is formed by adding an **s** to the singular form:

Un vélo neuf ***(a velo nuf)***	des vélos neufs***(a velo nuf)***
Une belle fleu ***(eun bel flo)***	des belle fleurs***(dez bel flo)***

Position of Adjectives:

However the following adjectives come before the noun:

Beau	***(bo)***
Bon	***(bon)***
Court	***(kourt)***
Grand	***(ghand)***
Gros	***(ghos)***
Haut	***(auth)***
Joli	***(jolee)***
Long	***(long)***
Mauvais	***(mauvaiz)***
Gentil	***(jauntil)***
Jeune	***(jaun)***
Méchant	***(mesho)***

Meilleur	***(maiyeur)***
Moindre	***(muandr)***
Petit	***(petit)***
Vieux	***(vayee)***
Villain	***(vlane)***

Some adjectives have a different meaning according to their position:

Adjective	**Before Noun**	**After Noun**
Ancient***(ancean)***	former	ancient
Brave(***bhav)***	good	brave
Certain***(cekhtan)***	some	sure
Cher***(sheh)***	dear	expensive
Dernier ***(dehneeyer)***	last, final	last
Grand(***ghnad)***	great	big, tall
Même ***(mem***)	same	very, selfsame
Pauvre ***(pauvr)***	poor(pitiable)	poor(not rich)
Proper(***propehr)***	own	clean
Seul(***sel)***	single, only	alone, lonely
Simple***(sample)***	mere	simple
Vrai (vraree)	real	true

Un brave type***(un brhave teeP)*** A nice guy	un homme brave a brave man
Chère john Dear John	un cadeau chère an expensive gift
Mon pauvre ami! My poor friend	Des gens pauvres poor people
Mon proper frère My own brother	une chamber proper a clean room
Un vrai casse-pieds A real bore	une histoire vraie a true story

Comparative and Superlative of Adjectives

1) the comparative form : more....than....less...than

2) the superlative form of the adjective: the most....,the least

plus...... que	more than
plus long	longer
plus cher	more expensive
moins......que	less than
moins long	less long
moins recent	less recent
aussi......que	as
aussi bon	as good
aussi important	as important

Note: .... This means placement of adjective

L'exercise:

A. Utilisez le adjectives á correct place :

1) Ila is a brave girl
2) This museum is very old
3) My friends's sister is very beautiful.
4) This book is not old
5) Stephanie is as beautiful as her sister.
6) These shoes are very expensive
7) Hotel " Wok Chok" is very old.
8) John is a gentil boy
9) I have mine own brother.
10) Where is the round table?
11) Where is the great man of our community?

Answers:

1) Ila est la fille brave.
   (ila a la fee brhave)
2) Cet muséum est très vieux.
   (say myuseum a thre veeaee)(
3) la sœur de mon ami est très belle.
   (la sir de maun amee a thre bel()
4) Cet livre n'est pas vieux.
   (cet leevr ne pas veeaee)

5) Stephanie est belle as aussi belle que sa sœur.
(Stephanie nab el a ausseebekl k sa sir)
6) Ces chausseurs sont plus cher.
(say shauser so plus sheh)
7) le Hôtel "Wok Chok" est très vieux.
(lotel "wok chok" a thre veeaee)
8) John est trè gentil garcon.
(John a thre jauntily gakhso)
9) J'ai mon proper frère.
(jai maun prohpr freh)
10) Où ést le round table.
(ou a le rond tabl)
11) Où est le grand homme.
(ou a le ghand om)

Le Leçon 12

Adverbs are normally used with a verb to express:

Manner
Time
Place
Intensity
Quantity

Adverbs of Manner: They are usually formed by adding –ment to the adjective(like –ly in English):

1) If the adjective ends in a consonant, **-ment** is added to its feminine form:

Adjective (masc, fem)	**Adverb**
doux, douce***(duus)***	doucement***(duusmo)***
franc,franche***(frankh, faunsh)***	franchement***(fanshmo)***
final,finale***(feenal)***	finalement***(feenalmo)***

2) If the adjective end in a vowel, **-ment** is added to it masculine

Adjective	**Adverb**
Absolu***(absolu)***	absolument***(absolumo)***
Désespéré(despeh)	désesperement***(despehmo)***
Vrai***(vraee)***	vraiment(***vreemo)***
Simple***(sampl)***	simplement***(samplmo)***

3) Some change the e of the feminine form of the adjective to é before adding **–ment:**

Adjective	**Adverb**
Commun***(commum)***	communément(***communmo)***
Précis***(precees***)	précisément ***(preecsmo)***

4) Some adverbs are completely irregular, including which are used very often.

Adjective	**Adverb**
Bon***(baun)***	Bien***(beaan)***
Bref***(bref)***	Brièvement***(brevemo)***
Gentil***(jauteel)***	Gentiment***(jaunteemo)***

Adverbs of Time - They are not formed from adjectives. Here are the commonest ones:

Alors**(aloh)**	then
Après***(apreh)***	afterwards
Aujourd'hui***(ohjudhuee)***	today
Aussitôt***(ositoh)***	right away, immediately
Bientôt ***(beantoh)***	soon
Encore***(oncor)***	still, again

Adverbs of Place- Here are the commonest ones:

Ailleurs***(ayeeyeh)***	somewhere else
Ici***(ici)***	here
Lá***(la)***	there
Loin***(luan)***	far away
Dessus***(dessu)***	on top, on it
Au-dessus***(au dessu)***	over,above
Dessous***(dessu)***	underneath
Au-dessous***(au dessu)***	below
Dedans***(dedaun)***	inside
Partout***(pakhtu)***	everywhere
Derrière ***(dehneeyer)***	behind

Adverbs of Intensity and Quantity:

Á piene***(a paan)***	hardly
Assez***(asse)***	enough, quite
Autant***(autant)***	as much/many
Beaucoup***(bucou)***	a lot, much / many
Comment ***(camò)***	how much / many
Moins***(muan)***	less

Plus***(plus)***	more
Presque***(prekh)***	almost
Peu***(p)***	little
Seulement***(selmo)***	only
Si***(see)***	if
Tant***(tau)***	so much/manhy
Tellement***(tellmo)***	so much/many
Très***(thre)***	very
Trop***(thro)***	too much
Un peu***(amp)***	a little

Note: Trop is usually use to give negative comment

All of these adverbs, except á peine, comme, Presque, si, très, seulment,

Comparative and Superlative of Adverbs

The comparative and superlative of adverbs are formed in the same was as adjectives:

Adverb	Comparative	Superlative
Souvent***(souvo)***	plus souvent que ***(plus souvo k)*** More often (than)	le plus souvent ***(plus souvo k)*** (the)most often
	Moins souvent(que) ***(mua souvo k)*** Less often(than)	le moins souvent ***(mua souvo k)*** (the) least often
	Aussi souvent(que)	***(aussee souvo)*** As often(as)

Note:

2) **as .... as possible** is translated either by **aussi...que possible or by le plus....possible**

as far as possible	aussi loin que possible ***(aussee lua k possibl)***

Le Leçon 13

Les Jours, Les Mois, les année, Le temp.

Le temp qui passé

Les jours en français, le genre du jours est masculine.

Days in English	**le Jour en français**
Monday	Lundi***(landee)***
Tuesday	Vendredi***(vathredee)***
Wednesday	Mardi***(makhdee)***
Thursday	Mercredi***(mekhredee)***
Friday	Jeudi***(jeudee)***
Saturday	Samedi***(samedee)***
Sunday	Dimanche***(deemaksh)***

Les mois en français, le genre de mois est masculine.

Months in French	**le mois en français** ***(le mua o francaiz)***
January	Janvier***(jaunveeer)***
February	Février***(fevreer)***
March	Mars***(maks)***
April	Avril***(avreel)***
May	Mai***(may)***
June	Juin***(juan)***
July	Juillet***(juee)***
August	Août***(ooth)***
September	Septembre***(septhombr)***
October	Octobre***(octobh)***
November	Novembre***(novaumbh)***
December	Décembre***(deesaumbh)***

Les Heures

Tu viens quand?*(tu veeyen kaun)*
-Je viens á huit heures.*(je veeyen a weeth a)*

Nous sommes quele jour?*(nouz som kel ju)*
On est quele jour?*(on a kel ju)*

- nous sommes mardi *(nooz som makhdee)*
- le 23 décembre *(le vint thua deeçaumbh)*

Quel date hier?*(kel data eehek)*
-Hier, c'etait 22 décembre.*(eehek, setait vint deux*

Pour demander l'heure:

Quelle heure est-il?*(kel a atil)*
Vous avez / tu as l'heure?*(voozave / tu a ler)*

Pour donner l'heure:

Il est quatorze heures trente*(eel a cathorz h thont)*

French doesn't have words for "a.m." and "p.m." You can use du matin for a.m., de l'après-midi from noon until 6p.m., and du soir from 6p.m. until midnight, but time is usually expressed on a 24-hour clock. Thus 3pm would be translated as quinze heures or 15h00.

In French, you have to say heure (except with midi and minuit), even though in English "o'clock" is often left out. In addition, the French hour and minute are separate by h (for heure) where in English we use a semi-colon :

Comment écris en français:

1) 45 minutes – moins le quart	*(mua le cath)*	(less fifteen)
2) 15 minutes – quart	*(cath)*	
3) 30 minutes- demie	*(deme)*	
4) 50 min – moin dix	*(mua dees)*	

What time is it? **Quelle heure est-il ?**

It's one o'clock	Il est une heure *(eel a eun a)*	1h00

It's two o'clock	Il est deux heures ***(eel a deux a)***	2h00
It's 3:30	Il est trois heures et demie ***(eel a thua a a demee)***	
	Il est trois heures trente ***(eel a thua a thont)***	3h30
It's 4:15	Il est quatre heures et quart ***(eel a cath a a cath)***	
	Il est quatre heures quinze ***(eel a cath a quinze)***	4h15
It's 4:45	Il est cinq heures moins le quart ***(eel a sunk a mua le cath)***	
	Il est cinq heures moins quinze ***(eel a sunk a mua quinz)***	
	Il est quatre heures quarante-cinq ***(eel a cath a cathorze sunk)***	4h45
It's 5:10	Il est cinq heures dix ***(eel a sunk a dees)***	5h10
It's 6:50	Il est sept heures moins dix ***(eel a seth a mua dees)***	
	Il est six heures cinquante ***(eel a seez a sunkont)***	6h50
It's 7am	Il est sept heures du matin ***(eel a seth a du mata)***	7h00
It's 3pm	Il est trois heures de l'après-midi ***(eel a thua a de laprehmeedee)***	

	Il est quinze heures ***(eel a quinze a)***	15h00
It's 6pm	Il est six heures du soir ***(eel a seez a du sua)***	
	Il est dix-huit heures ***(eel a dees weet a)***	18h00
It's noon	Il est midi ***(eel a meedee)***	12h00
It's midnight	Il est minuit ***(eel a meenuee)***	0h00

Learn how to write dates in full:

3.5.1953 - le trios mai mille neuf cinquante trios
(le thua may meel nuf sunkont thua)
27.8.1995 – le vingt sept âout mille neuf quatre vingt qunize
(le v seth out meel nuf cathr v canz)
15.12.1962 - le qunize décembre mille neuf soixante deux
(le canz deesaumbh meel nuf suasaont d)

French Time

Second	Seconde***(seecond)***
Minute	Minute***(meenuee)***
Hour	Heure***(a)***
Day	Jour***(ju)***
Week	Semaine***(seemain)***
Year	Année***(annee)***
Yesterday	Hier***(ehek)***
Today	Aujourd'hu***(ojourdhuee0i***
Tomorrow	Demain***(dema)***
Last week	la semaine dernier***(le semain derhneeyer)***
Next month	la mois prochain***(la mua prshain)***
Early	Tôt***(toh)***

Note: Dates are always followed by **"Le"**

Il est midi
(eel a meedee) It is midday.

Á minuit.
(a minuee) At midnight.

Je commence á huit heures trente ***(huit heures et demie).***
(je cmmaunce a weet a thont) I begin at 8.30.

Je termine á trois heures trente
(je tehminee a thua a thont) I finish at half past three.

Je suis en retard.
(je suee o retarhd) I'm late.

Est ce que je suis trop tôt ?
(esk je suee thro to) Am I too early ?

Il y a douze mois dans l'année
(eelyą dooz mua danz lannee) There are twelve months in a year

Il est exactement trios heures.
(eel a exactmo thua a) It is exactly three o'clock.

Á onze heures précises
(a oonz a preceese) At eleven sharp.

montre est á l'heure?
(montr a a lz) Is this clock right?

Dans deux heures
(danz d a) In two hours.

Elle avance(retarde)
(l avans) (rethard) It's too fast(slow)

Mercredi en Huii ***(mekhredi a wheat)***	A week from Wednesday
Dans une semaine ***(danz eun semain)***	A week from now.
Pendant la journée. ***(paundo la journe)***	During the day time.
Avant-hier. ***(avo ehek)***	The day before yesterday
Pas avant sept heures. ***(pa avo seth a)***	Not before seven.
Dans les huit jours ***(danz lez wheat jou)***	Within a week.
La week-end prochain! ***(la weekon proshain)***	This coming weekend

Séason!

Spring	printemps(m) ***(prontom)***
Summer	été (m) ***(ate)***
Fall/Autumn	automne(m) ***(otom)***
Winter	hiver (m) ***(ehver)***
Good Friday	Vendredi saint ***(venthredi saint)***
Faster	pâques ***(pak)***
Christmans	Noël(m) ***(noyel)***

Rendez vous á paris !

Chér John,

Quc se passe-t-il?Nous n'avons pas de nouvelles. J'éspere tu as très bien.Quels sont vos projets?Quand arrives tu á Paris.?Le 23 juin je vais á Luzembourg.

Est-ce que tu n'as pas partir en vacances avec ton ami Stephanie pour 3 jours?Mais avant nous attendons votre visite. Merci de téléphoner ou d'écrire rapidement.

Amitiés

Stephanie

(sheh john,

J say pastil?nooz navo pad de nouvel. Nooz navo pa de novel.Jespeh tu a thre beea. Kel so vo projet?Kaun arrheeve tu a pahi?I v thua jua je vay a luzembugh.

Esk tu na pa pkahit on vaconz avez taun amee Stephanie pour thua jou?Mein avo nooz attondo vothr veeseet/ Mehsi de telephone ou deckhree raphidmo

Ameeteeye

Stephanie)

Le Leçon 14

La Météo

Anglais	**Français**
the weather	le temps (m) or la météo (f) ***(le taump) (la meteeo)***
the weather forecast	le bulletin météo (m) or la météo (f) ***(le bulleten meteeo)(la meeteo)***
the sun	le soleil (m) ***(le solee)***
the cloud	le nuage (m) ***(le nuaage)***
the sky	le ciel (m) ***(le seal)***
the rain	la pluie (f) ***(la pluee)***
the wind	le vent (m ***(le vo)***

the storm	la tempête (f)
	(le taumpet)
the thunder	l'orage (m)
	(lohage)
the flash of lightning	l'éclair (m)
	(leclair)
the rainbow	l'arc-en-ciel (m)
	(larc o seeal)

And concerning temperatures:

Anglais	**Français**
the heat	la chaleur (f)
	(la shaleur)
the cold	le froid (m)
	(la fuhad)
the temperature	la température (f)
	(la temperature)
the degree	le degré (m)
	(le degree)

Pour Parler du temps qu'il fait:

Il fait chaud !
(eel feh sho) *It's hot!*

Quelle chaleur !
(kel shaleur) *It's boiling!*

It fait doux. or Il fait bon.
(eel feh douce or eel feh baun) *It's warm.*

Il fait soleil. or Il fait beau or Il ya du soleil
(eel feh solee or eel feh Baun or eelya du solee) *It's sunny.*

Il pleut. (future: Il pleuvra.)
(eel pl) *It's raining.*

Il fait froid.
(eel feh fuhad) — *It's cold.*

La température a monté (baissé) de 10 degrés.
(la temperature a montee de dees degree) — *The temperature has risen (fallen) by 10 degrees.*

Il y a beaucoup de nuages dans le ciel.
(eelya bucou de nuhag danz le seal) — *There are lots of clouds in the sky.*

Le temps est nuageux.
(le taum a nuhag) — *It's a cloudy weather.*

La météo est mauvaise.
(la meteo a mauvaiz) — *Weather is bad.*

Le soleil brille.
(la solee bheel) — *The sun shines.*

Quel brouillard!
(kel bhuiyaad) — How foggy it is !

Qual soleil!
(kel solee) — How sunny it is !

Quel vent!
(kel vo) — How windy it is !

Quell froid!
(Kel fuhad) — How cold it is !

J'ai froid / chaud!
(jai fuhad / sho) — I am feeling cold / hot

Il y a du verglas
(eelya du vehglas) — Its very slippery.

La Météo du 30 Aôut :

Il est très chaud et le soleil brille sur toute la France. Cet aprè midi, la temperature de 29 á 34 degrés du nord au sud. En fin de journée, quelques coup la tempête et l'oranges dans le Sud-ouest. Au nuit il ya le chance du pluie. Si Vous allez ailleurs, n'oubliez pas le parapluie.

(eel a thre sho de le solee bheel sur tut la fonce. Cet aprhe meedee, la temperature de vingt neuf a trente quatre degree du nohd o sud. O fa de journee, kelk cou la tempet a lohange danz le syud west. O nuee eelya le chaanse du pluee. See vooz alle iyer, nublee pa le parapluee.)

L'exercise

A. Traduiez en français;

In South of France it is raining and strom badly, there are the chances of the rain in North East also. At some of the places in France sun is shining and no chances of bad weather. In West of France it is remain as foggy and will become cold at night.

Answers:

A. En Sud de France il fait neige et la têmpete guère, aussi il y a du chances de neige en Nord-Est. En France á quel que place il fait soleil et il n'y a pas le météo est mauvais. En Ouest de France il rests comme brouillard et deviens froid a nuit.

(on syud de fonce il feh nej a la taumpet gueh, aussee eelya du shance de nej on Nohd—Est. O Fonce a kel k plas el feh solee a eela pa le meteeo a mauvaiz. On oust de Fonce eel resth kom bouhiyaad a deveeya fuhad a nuee)

Le Leçon 15

La Cuisine
Ustensils de Cuisine

Bottle	Boutcillc (f)***(butaiile)***
Bowl	Terrine(f)***(teheen)***
Cup	Tasse(f) ***(tas)***
Saucer	Soucoupe(f)***(socou)***
Cutlery	Couvert (m)***(couveht)***
Fork	Fourchette(f) ***(fouhshet)***
Glass	Verre (m)***(veh)***
Water glass	Verre à eau (m) ***(veh a o)***

Vine glass	Verre á vin(m) ***(veh a vin)***
Knife	Couteau (m) ***(couto)***
Napkin	Serviette(f) ***(sehveeyet)***
Plate	Assiette(f) ***(asseyet)***
Bread plate	Petite assisette(f) ***(peteet asseyet)***
Soup Plate	Assiette á soupe (f) (***asseyet a soup)***
Spoon	Cuiller(f) ***(keyeh)***
Soup spoon	Cuiller a soupe(f) ***(keyeh a soup)***
Table cloth	Nappe (f***) (naap)***
Toothpick	Cure dent(m) ***(kyuh do)***
Tray	Plateau (m) ***(plato)***
Serving dish	Plat (m)(***pla)***

Le petite dejeuner (breakfast)
(le peteet dejeunay)

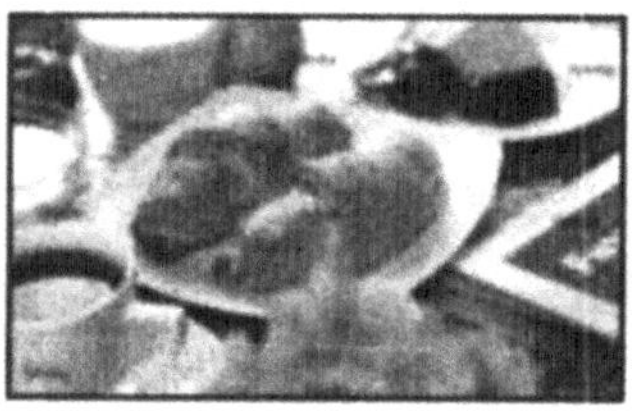

Bread	pain(m) ***(pain)***
Butter	Beurre (m) ***(beh)***
Coffee	Café(m) ***(café)***
Coffee with cream	café au lait(m) (***café o lai)***
Egg	œuf(m) ***(of)***
Hard boiled eggs	œuf dur(m) ***(of duh)***
Fruit juice	jus de fruits (m) ***(jus de fuee)***
Orange juice	Jus de orange (m) ***(jus d ohang)***
Honey	Miel(m) ***(meel)***
Jam	Confiture (f) ***(confeetu)***
Milk	Lait(m) ***(leh)***
Tea	Thé (m) ***(the)***
Tea with milk	Thé au lait(m) ***(the o leh)***
Lemon	Citron(m) ***(cithron)***

Les ingrédients

Butter	Beurre(m) ***(beh)***
Cinnamon	Cannelle(f) ***(cannel)***
Garlic	Ail (m) ***(ail)***
Ginger	Gingembre(m)***(geegaumbh)***
Ketchup	Ketchup(m) ***(kechup)***
Mushrooms	Champignons(m) ***(shampeeno)***
Mustard	Moutarde (f) ***(moohad)***
Oil	Huile(f) ***(hue)***
Olives	Olives (f) ***(oleeve)***
Onion	Oignon(m) ***(oniyon)***
Pepper	Poivre (m) ***(puhavr)***
Pickels	Cornichons(m) ***(cohneeshau)***
Raisins	Raisins (m) ***(raisins)***
Salt	Sel (m)***(cell)***
Sauce	Sauce (m) ***(sauce)***
Vanilla	Vanille (f)***(vaneel)***
Vinegar	Vinaigre (m)***(veenehgre)***

Les legumes

Carrots	Carottes (f)***(cahott)***
Cabbage	Chou (m)***(shu)***
Cauliflower	Chou-fleur (m)***(shu fleur)***
Cucumber	Concombre (m)***(concaumbh)***
Pumpkin	Courge (f)***(kouhag)***
Spinach	Epinards (m)***(apeenahd)***
Beans	Haricots (m)***(aheecot)***
Peas	Petits pois (m)***(peteet puha)***
Potatoes	Pommes de terre (f)***(paum de the)***
Mashed potatoes	Pommes de mousseline (f) ***(paum de moozeleen)***
French Fries	Pommes de frites***(paum de free0***
Salad	Salade(f)***(salad)***
Tomatoes	Tomates(f) ***(taumat)***

Les Fruites

Pineapple	Ananas (m)***(anaanaas)***
Almonds	Amandes (f)***(amand)***
Banana	Banane(f)***(banan)***
Black Currants	Cassis (m)***(case)***
Coconut	Coco (m)***(coca)***
Dates	Dattes (f)***(data)***
Strawberries	Fraises (f)***(frehz)***
Rasberries	Framboises (f)***(fhambuasees)***
Orange	Orange (f)***(ohanz)***
Peach	Pêch (m)***(pesh)***
Pear	Poire f)***(puah)***
Apple	Pomme (f)***(paum)***
Grapes	Raisins (m)***(raiseenz0***

Les Boissons (f)

Brandy	Eau de vie (f)***(o de va)***
Gin	Gin (m)***(geen)***
Lemonade	Limonade (f)***(lemonade)***
Juice	Jus de orange (m)***(juz de ohanz)***
Water	Eau (f)***(o)***

Dans le café

In France, as in most of Europe, a café is a great place to relax with a cup of coffee, meet friends, read the paper or most popular of all people watch.

Je voudrais ou Je voudrais commandender

A piece of cake	un morceau de gateau ***(a mokhso de gato)***
A cup of coffee	un café ***(a café)***
A cup of tea	un thé ***(a the)***
A dish of icecream	une galce ***(eun glass)***
A glass of orange juice	un verre de jus d'orange ***(a veh de juz dohanz)***

Chocolate	chocolat (m) ***(shokokala)***
Confectionary	Pâtisserie (f) ***(pateeseree)***
Strawberry icecream	glace á la fraise ***(glass a la frez)***
Vanilla icecream	glace á la vanilla ***(glas a la vaneela)***
Ice cream parlour	Pâtissier glacier ***(pateeseree glacear)***
Cold milk	lait froid ***(leh fuhad)***
Sherbet	sorbet (m) ***(sorbeh)***
Sugar	sucre (m) ***(sucree)***
Cube sugar	sucre en morceau ***(sucree a mokhso)***
Sweets	Bonbons (m) ***(baunbaun)***
Tart	Tarte (f) ***(taht)***
Wafers	gaufrettes ***(gaufreht)***

This isn't what I ordered.
Je n'ai pas commandé cela.
(je ne pas kmaund sela)

This is not fresh anymore
Ce n'est pas plus frais
(ce ne pas plus frez)

Too fatty	trop gras ***(thro ghas)***
Too hard	trop dur ***(thro duh)***
Too hot	trop chaud ***(thro sho)***

Too spicy	trop épicé
	(thro apiece)
Too salty	trop sale
	(thro sale)
Too sour	trop aigre
	(thro aigr)

Vous visitez au restaurant avec vos amis, veuillez troives les dialogues entre vous et garcon qui travail.

Garçon: Bonjour Messieus, est ce que vous voules la carte ou le menu?
(bonju messeyur, esk vooz voule le cakht ou le menu)

Vous : Bonjour, la carte sil vous plait!
(bonju, la cakht seel vooz play)

Garçon: Biensûr.
(beansuh)

Vous: Je voudaris le sandwhich, un verre de orange
(je voudre le sondweech, un veh dohanz)

Garçon: D'accord et vos amis
(dhaco a voz amee)

Vous : deux café sans sucre, trios tarte aux fruits et un sandwhich de tomatoes
(deux café sao sucree, thua takht o fuee a un sonweech de taumat)

Garçon: Çava !
(sava)

Garçon: C'est votre menu
(say vothr menu)

Vous: Excusez moi! Ce n'est plus frais
(excuseze mua, c ne pas plus frez)

Garçon: pas de problem! Je remplace immediatement.
(pas de problem! Je raumplasay immeegiakhtmo)

Vous: une salade de crudités aussi.
(eun salad de j\khudeete ossi)

Garçon : vous devez essayer le possion et le morceau de froamge?
(vooz deve asayee le puazon a le mokhso de fhomaz)

Vous: C'est une bonne idée.
(satune bau eedee)

Vous: C'est trop chaud!
(say thro sho)

Garçon: Quelque chose ?
(kelkchose)

Vous: No merci! L'addition sil vous plait!
(no mehsee!laadeecion seel vooz play)

Vous: Ce ne pas me paraît.
(ce ne pas me pahait)

Garçon: desolée! Est ce que vous voulez?
(dezolee!esk vooz voule)

Vous: Je paie tout! C'est pour vous!
(je pay tout! Cest pur vooz)

Garçon: Merci mille fois!
(mehsi meel fua)

Le Leçon 16

Age

J'ai vingt ans. ***(jai v onz)***	I am 20 yrs old.
J'ai plus de dix-huit ans. ***(jai plus de dees weet onz)***	I'am over 18 yrs old.
Enfants au dessous de quatorze ans. ***(onfo u dessu de cathorz onz)***	Children under 14 yrs old.
Il est plus jeune (plus sage) ***(8eel a plus jung)***	He is younger (older).
Je suis né le ***(je suee nai le)***	I was born on the.
Mineur ***(miner)***	Under age
Adulte ***(aadoult)***	Adult
Á l'âge de .... Ans ***(a laaz de on)***	At the age of ....
Á mon âge de ***(a maun anz de)***	At my age of .

Body parts

Arm	bras (m)***(bha)***
Back	dos(m)***(do)***
Blood	sang(m)***(sang)***
Body	corps(m)***(cohp)***
Bone	os(m)***(oz)***
Brain	cerveau(m)***(cehvo)***
Breast	poitrine (f)***(poitreen)***
Chest	poitrine(f ***(poitreen)***
Chin	menton (m) ***(mento)***
Digestion	digestion (f)***(dyegescio)***
Ear	oreille(f) ***(oheel)***
Elbow	coude(m) ***(coohad)***
Eye	œil (yeux)***(yex)***
Face	visage (m) ***(veesaz)***
Finger	doigt (m) ***(dua)***
Thumb	pouce (m)***(puus)***
Foot	pied (m)***(peeh)***
Forehead	front(m)***(fonth)***
Hair	cheveux (m)***(shv)***
Hand	main (f)***(mai)***
Heart	cœur(m)***(cur)***
Hip	hanche (f)***(ansh)***
Leg	jambe (f0***(jaumb)***
Thigh	cuisse (f)***(cuees)***
Mouth	bouche (f)***(bush)***
Muscle	muscle (f)***(muuscl)***
Nail	ongle (m)***(ongl)***
Nose	nez (m)***(nez)***
Penis	pénis (m)***(pehnees)***
Shoulder	épaule (f)***(apaul)***
Stomach	estomac (m)***(astomak)***
Throat	gorge (f)(***gohz)***
Tongue	langue(f) ***(laung)***
Tooth	dent (m)***(dau)***
Urin	urine (f) ***(uheen)***
Uterus	utorus (m)***(utherus)***
Vagina	vagin (m)***(vageen)***

Le Leçon 17

Tense

Tense refers to one of 8 verb forms which express the time and completion (or lack thereof) of the verb's action or condition.

Tenses

Présent	Present	
Imparfait	Imperfect	
Passé simple	Simple	Past
Plus-que-parfait	Present	Perfect
Passé antérieur	Past	Perfect
Futur	Future	
Futur antérieur	Future Perfect	

In all the earlier chapters we have been using the present tense but now we will explain you in this chapter that what exactly is the meaning and the time where this tense can be used.

Présent

Usage of the Present

When you want to talk about something that's happening now.

Formation of the Present

To form the present tense, there are seven categories of verbs that you need to know about, sorted by their endings, and if they are regular (follow the rules) or irregular (have their own rules).

They are:

- -er verbs
- -ir verbs
- -re verbs
- irregular -er verbs
- irregular -ir verbs
- irregular -re verbs
- really really irregular verbs

Regular Verbs

Regular -er Verbs

- For non stem-changing regular -er verbs, the stem is determined by removing the final -er.
- After determining the stem, conjugate by adding the appropriate endings.

Subject	Ending
je	-e
tu	-es
il	-e
nous	-ons
vous	-ez
ils	-ent

e.g. Parler

Je	parle
Tu	parles
Il/Elle	parle
Nous	parlons
Vous	parlez
Ils/Elles	parlent

Conjugation of Regular -ir Verbs

- For regular -ir verbs, the stem is determined by removing the final -ir.
- After determining the stem, conjugate by adding the appropriate endings.

Subject	Ending
je	-is
tu	-is
il	-it
nous	-issons
vous	-issez
ils	-issent

e.g Finir

Je	finis
Tu	finis
Il/Elle	finit
Nous	finissons
Vous	finissez
Ils/Elles	finnissent

Conjugation of Regular -re Verbs

- For regular -re verbs, the stem is determined by removing the final -re.
- After determining the stem, conjugate by adding the appropriate endings.

Subject	Ending
je	-s
tu	-s

il	-(no additons)
nous	-ons
vous	-ez
ils	-ent

e.g. Prendre

Je	prends
Tu	prends
Il/Elle	prend
Nous	prenons
Vous	prenez
Ils/Elles	prenent

Irregular Conjugations

- Several verbs are irregularly conjugated in the present.
- Some verbs can be categorized by the general pattern they follow, while others are completely irregular.
- Irregular verbs are too numerous to be entirely provided here. Only some common irregular verbs will be shown.

Stem Changing -er Verbs

- Several French verbs are stem-changing; the endings for conjugation basically remain the same, but slight changes occur with the stem.
- One may divide the category of stem-changing verbs into two subcategories: verbs whose stems change only in the nous form and verbs whose stems change only in the je, tu, il, and ils forms.

-cer Verbs

- To conjugate a -cer verb in the nous form, change the c **a** or an **o to preserve the soft sound of the** c.
- Conjugations in the je, tu, il, vous, and ils forms remain unaffected.

e.g. Commencer

Je	commence***(kmaunse)***
Tu	commences ***(kmaunse)***
Il/elle	commence ***(kmaunse)***
Nous	commençons ***(kmaunso)***
Vous	commencez ***(kmaunsez)***
Ils/Elles	commencent ***(kmaunso)***

-ger Verbs

- To conjugate a -ger verb in the nous form, add an e between the final g and the ending ons.
- Conjugations in the je, tu, il, vous, and ils forms remain unaffected.

e.g Changer

Je	change ***(shanz)***
Tu	changes ***(shanz)***
Il/Elle	change ***(shanz)***
Nous	changeons ***(shanzeo)***
Vous	changez ***(shanze)***
Ils/Elles	changent ***(shanzo)***

-ayer, -oyer, and -uyer Verbs

- To conjugate an -ayer, -oyer, or -uyer verb in the je, tu, il, and ils forms, change the y to i.
- Conjugations in the nous and vous forms remain unaffected.

e.g. Envoyer

Je	envoie ***(onvoy)***
Tu	envoies ***(onvoy)***
Il/Elle	envoie ***(onvoy)***

Nous	envoyons ***(onvoyo)***
Vous	envoyez ***(onvoye)***
Ils/Elles	envoyent ***(onvoyo)***

e.g. Essayer

Je	essaie ***(assay)***
Tu	essaies ***(assay)***
Il/elle	essaie ***(assay)***
Nous	essayons ***(assayo)***
Vous	essayez ***(assaye)***
Ils/Elles	essayent ***(assayo)***

-eler Verbs

- To conjugate an -eler verb in the je, tu, il, and ils forms, change the l to ll.
- Conjugations in the nous and vous forms remain unaffected.

e.g. Appeller

J'	appelle ***(appel)***
Tu	appelles ***(appel)***
Il/Elle	appelle ***(appel)***
Nous	appelons ***(appelo)***
Vous	applez ***(appelez)***
Ils/Elles	appellent ***(appelo)***

-eter Verbs

- To conjugate an -eter verb in the je, tu, il, and ils forms, change the t to tt.
- Conjugations in the nous and vous forms remain unaffected.

e.g. Jeter

Je	jette ***(jet)***
Tu	jettes ***(jet)***
Il/Elle	jette ***(jet)***
Nous	jetons ***(jeto)***
Vous	jetez ***(jete)***
Ils/Elles	jettent ***(jeto)***

Verbs with e in the second to last syllable

- To conjugate a verb with an e in the second to last syllable in the je, tu, il, and ils forms, change the e to è.
- Conjugations in the nous and vous forms remain unaffected.

Verbs with é in the second to last syllable

- To conjugate a verb with an é in the second to last syllable in the je, tu, il, and ils forms, change the é to è.
- Conjugations in the nous and vous forms remain unaffected.

Irregular -ir Verb Patterns

Couvrir

- The verbs couvrir, cueillir, offrir, ouvrir, and souffrir, follow this pattern.
- The stem is determined by removing the final -ir.
- Although the verbs are -ir verbs, they are treated like regular -er verbs for the purpose of conjugation. Thus, they utilize the regular endings for -er verbs.

Dormir

- The verbs dormir, mentir, partir, sentir, servir, and sortir follow this pattern.
- For conjugating the plural forms (nous, vous, ils), the stem is determined by removing the final -ir.
- For conjugating the singular forms (je, tu, il), the stem is the same as the plural stem, except that the last letter of the plural stem is removed in addition to the -ir.
- The verb ending pattern for these verbs is as follows:

Le Leçon 18

Imperfect tense – Imparfait

Usage of the Imperfect

The imperfect is a past tense used to express what someone was doing or what someone used to do, or to describe something in the past. The imperfect refers particularly to something that continued as opposed to something that happened at a specific point in time. The imperfect is used:

- To refer to previously ongoing and repeated events that are now completely finished.
- To express an action that happened often in the past, such as a habit that one has grown out of. For example, "I **used to eat** a kiwi while watching the news." is in French, "Je **mangeais** un kiwi en regardant les informations."
- In describing the past, including things such as: time, location, weather, age, physical appearance, physical and emotional conditions or states, attitudes and desires and other mental experiences.
- Actions that occured while something else was happening.
- To compare and contrast events in the present with events in the past.
- To talk about the emotions or abstract qualities of a person/thing in the past or to discuss an irritating quality or subject.
- To suggest or ask certain "forceful" questions such as, "Si on faisait une promènade?"
- When phrases like I used to do... and I would do... are used in English.

Formation of the Imperfect

Imperfect Stem

- For all verbs except for être, the imperfect stem is determined by removing the -ons from the nous form of the present indicative of the verb.
- Certain verbs (-cer and -ger verbs) are stem-changing in the nous form of the present indicative; these are stem-changing the imperfect also. The stem change that applies in the present indicative is retained when conjugating the je, tu, il, and ils forms of the imperfect. That stem change is reversed when conjugating the nous and vous forms of the imperfect.
- For être, the imperfect stem is ét-.

Imperfect Ending

- To conjugate in the imperfect, add the appropriate ending to the imperfect stem.

Subject	Ending
je	-ais
tu	-ais
il	-ait
nous	-ions
vous	-iez
ils	-aient

Examples

Aller

Subject	Ending
j'	allais
tu	allais
il	allait
nous	allions
vous	alliez
ils	allaient

Être

Subject	**Ending**
j'	étais
tu	étais
il	était
nous	étions
vous	étiez
ils	étaient

e.g.

1) Continuous actions: When something else took place.

Elle regardait le television quand je lui a appelé
(el regarhd le television kaun je luee a appele)
She was watching television when I called her.

Excusez-moi, je pensais á autre chose.
(excusez mua, je paunse a authr shose)
Excuse me, I was thinking of someone else.

2) Regular actions in the past:

Je le voyait souvent quand il habitait dans le quartier.
(je le voyez souvo kaun eel abet danz le katheeyer)
I used to see him when he was staying in the neighbour.

Quand il etait plus jeune il voyageait beaucoup.
(kaun eel feh plus jeun eel voyajay bucou)
When he was very young he used to traveled a lot.

3) Description in the past:

Il faisait beau ce jour lá.
(eel fasaiz bo se jou la)
The weather was good that day.

Elle etait trop grosse.
I(el etay thro ghoss)
She was very fat.

Je aimait le banana.
(je aimay le banan)
I used to like banans

Le Leçon 19

Passé composé - The passé composé is a perfect tense, and is therefore composed of an auxiliary verb and a past participle. With most verbs, that auxililary verb is avoir.It is usually used to express that event which was already completed in the past.

In English, verbs conjugated in the passé composé literally mean have/ has ____ed. While there is a simple past tense in French, it is only used in formal writing, so verbs conjugated in the passé composé can also be used to mean the English simple tense.

- For example, the passé composé form of parler (to speak), [avoir] parlé, literally mean has/have spoken, but also means spoke. In French, the passé composé covers "I ate", "I did eat" and "I have eaten" - J'ai mangé.

When to use

You use the passé composé when you want to express that:

1. Something has been completed in the past.
2. Something was done a certain amount of times in the past. (if the something was ongoing, the imparfait should be used)
3. A series of somethings was completed in the past.

Formation

Introduction

To conjugate a verb in the passé composé, the auxiliary (or helping) verb, usually avoir, is conjugated in the present indicative and the past participle is then added. **It is important to remember that there is only *one* verb in the passé composé**. While the past participle looks like a verb, it is not - it functions more like an adjective. This is is important to remember because when you negate in the passé composé, you negate the only verb, which is the auxiliary verb (ex. "Je n'ai pas mangé"; "I have not eaten").

This works exactly the same way in English - the only verb is the auxiliary verb, which is also the only thing negated in English ("I have not eaten").

Formation Summary

The compound past is a compound tense- it consists of two verbs, the auxiliary verb ("helper verb") and the past participle of the verb one seeks to use in this tense.

To form the passé composé, you need to take the auxiliary verb - either avoir (or être for irregular verbs), then make it agree with the subject of the sentence, like in the present indicative tense. We then take the past participle of the verb, and stick that on the end. Every verb has one past participle that does not change (there are some exceptions, as one will learn later). To find the past participle, the stem of the infinitive must be determined. To do so, drop the -er, -ir, -oir or -re, as usual.

If we want to make the statement negative, for example if we didn't do something in the past, we must always put the negative structure such as ne ... pas around the auxiliary verb, immediately before the past participle. For example, "Je ne peux pas",.

Also, reflexive or pronomial verbs must be conjugated with être under most circumstances. For example, the verb "se reflechir" is conjugated in the first person singular by "Je me suis reflechi,".

Auxiliary Verb Formation

- The auxiliary verb is always either avoir or être.
- The tense of the verb depends upon the tense that avoir or être is conjugated in.
    - When the auxiliary verb is conjugated in the passé composé, for example, the auxiliary verb is conjugated in the present indicative.
        - J'ai fini. - I have finished.

Auxiliary Verb - Être

Conjugate être in the present indicative.

je	suis
tu	es

il	est
nous	sommes
vous	êtes
ils	sont

Past Participle Formation

- **-er** verbs - replace -er with é
- **-ir** verbs - replace -ir with i
- **-re** verbs - replace -re with u
- irregular verbs - must be memorized

Verb Group	Infinitive	Stem	Past Participle
-er verbs	jou**er**	jou	jou**é**
-ir verbs	fin**ir**	fin	Fin**i**
-re verbs	répond**re**	répond	répond**u**

Avoir + Past Participle

Jouer

J'	ai	joué
Tu	as	joué
Il/Elle	a	joué
Nous	avons	joué
Vous	avez	joué
Ils/Elles	ont	joué

Être + Past Participle

In this case, if the conjugation is of the feminine, then addition of e in singular and es in plural is required. Please see the example below.

Je suis allé(e).	I went.
(je suee allay)	
Tu es allé(e).	You went.
(tu as allay)	
Il/On est allé.	He went.
(eel / on a allay)	
Elle est allée.	She went.
(el a allay)	
Nous sommes allé(e)s.	we went
(nooz zom allay)	
Vous êtes allé(e)(s).*	you (all) went
Ils sont allés.	they went
(eels zo allaY0	
Elles sont allées.	they went
(el zo allay)	

- Note that for the starred vous form, the S (which is always added for nous and ils/elles) is not added if the vous is simply denoting the singular, formal you.

Past Participle Agreement with Preceding Direct Objects

The past participle must agree with the direct object of a clause in gender and plurality if the direct object goes before the verb.

- the direct object is masculine singular - no change
  - J'ai fini le jeu - I have finished the game.
    (jai feenee le jo).
  - Je l'ai fini. - I have finished it.
    (jai leh feenee)
- the direct object is feminine singular - add an **e** to the past participle
  - J'ai fini la tâche. - I have finished the task.
    (jai feenee la tash)
  - Je l'ai finie. - I have finished it.
    (jai leh feenee)
- the direct object is masculine plural - add an **s** to the past participle.
  - J'ai fini les jeux. - I have finished the games.
    (jai feenee le jo)

- Je les ai finis. - I have finished them.
  (je lez a feenee)

- the direct object is feminine plural - add an **es** to the past participle.
  - J'ai fini les tâches. - I have finished the tasks.
    (jai feenee lez tash)
  - Je les ai finies. - I have finished them.
    (je lez a feenee)

Avoir ou Être?

In most circumstances, the auxiliary verb is avoir. However, with certain verbs, the auxiliary verb is être. This occurs under two different circumstances:

1. **The House of Être:** Most verbs form the passé composé with avoir, however there are a small number of verbs that are always conjugated with être. Seventeen special intransitive verbs take être. If you want to form the negative sentence then **ne.... pas verb. E.g. ne suis pas allé**

Verbs that take Être in the passé composé

1)Arriver – to arrive

Je suis arrivé hier á 10 heures du matin.
(je suee arrheeve a dix a du mata) I arrived yesterday at 10 am.

Nous sommes arrivés á la bibliothèque
(nooz zom arreeheeve a la beeblotheck) We arrived at the library.

2)Mourir – to die.

Lynnette est morte en 1917.
(lyneet a morht a 1917) Lynnette died in 1917.

Je suis mort á cause des examen.
(je suee mokht a cauz dez exama) I died because of my exams.

3) Aller – to go

Est ce que elles ont allées au chez de Lynnette?
(esl elzo alle o chez de lynet) Did they go at Lynnette's house?

Ju suis allé au restaurant. ***(je suee alle o resthoro)***	I went to the restaurant.

4) Venir – to come

Il est venu á chez moi pour etudie. ***(eel a venu a chez mua´ pur atudyee)***	He came to my house for studies.
Toute les enfants sont venu ici. ***(tut lezonfo so venu ici)***	All the children came here

5)Devenir – to become

Je suis devenu la professeur de Français. ***(je suee devnu la professeur de foncais)***	I became the professor of French.
Tu est devenue trop mince. ***(tu a devenue thro mance)***	you became very weak.

6)Rentre : to re-enter or go back to home.

Je suis rentré de chez mon ami. ***(je suee rauntr de chez maun amee)***	I came back from my friend's home
Il est entré de le bureau. ***(eel a onthre de le buro)***	He returned from the office.

7) Sortir – to go out

Je suis sorti ce soir. ***(je suee sokhti ce sua)***	I left that evenning.
Est –ce que nous sommes sortis du fête plus tard? ***(esk nooz zom sokhti du teth plus tahd)***	They left from the party early?

8) Partir – to leave.

Elle est parti pour travilleur.

(el a pakhti pur thavaiye)	She left for the work.

Je suis parti pour l'aéroport á 9 heures.

(je suee pakhti pur le ahopokht a neuh a)	I left for the airport at 9'o clock.

Meanings of sortir and partir are almost same but only the difference is when we use "Sortir" it means to leave the place permanently and when we use "Partir" it means to leave the place but then there are chance of return to the same place.

9) Revenir- to come back again

Je suis revenue dans cette salle pour chercher mon cahier.

(je suee revenue danz cet saal pur shehshe maun caheeyer)	I came back to this room to find my notebook.

Il est venu du fête.

(eel a venu du feth)	He came back from the party.

10) Retourner – to return to same place from where have you come

Je suis retourné(e) au café le lendemain.

(je suee rethourne u café le laundema)	I went back to the café the next day.

Il est retourné au restaurant.

(eel a rethourne o resthoro)	I returned to the restaurant

11) Nâltre- to born

Je suis né á Delhi.

(je suee ne a daily)	I born in Delhi.

Il est né le 27 Janvier en 1984.

(eel a ne le vingt sept jaunveeyer au 1984)	He was born on January 27 in 1984.

12) Descendre – to come down

Je suis descendu du vélo.

(j suee descendu du veedeo) I cam down from the cycle.

Nous sommes descendu des escaliers.

(nooz zom descendu dez sclaiyer) We came down from the stairs.

13) Monter- to climb

Je suis monté la voiture.

(ju suee monte la vachyu) I climbed the trees.

Vous êtes montée dans la voiture de l'école.

(vooz zet monte danz la vachyu de lecol) You climbed the school bus.

14) Entre – to enter

Je suis entré en retarde.

(je suee antre o rethard) I entered very late.

Ils sont entré le cinéma á temps.

(eel zo antre la ceenema a taump) They entered the cinemà on time.

15) Tomber – to fall

Je suis tombé mon ami de l'abre.

(je suee taumbe maun amee de labh) I fell down my friend from the tree.

Il est tombé de sa chaise.

(eel a taumbe de sa chaiz) He fell down from the chair.

16) Rester – to stay(not to rest)

Je suis restée avec ma ami en Paris pour 3 ans.

(je suee resthe avec ma amee o pahee pur trois ons) I stayed with my friend in Paris for 3 yrs.

Est-ce que tu est resté chez toi vendredi soir?

(esk tu a resthe chez tua venthredi sua) Did you stayed at your home on Friday evening.

17) Passer – to pass by

Je suis passé par le bibliothéque.

(je suee passee pah le beeblotheck) I passed by from the library.

Il est passé devant la maison.

(eel a passé devaht la maizon) It happened in front of the house.

1.a. Exceptions Note that there are four verbs above that are followed by a star (sortir, descendre, monter, passer). When a direct object is used with these verbs, the auxillary verb becomes avoir.

Être Verbs that take Avoir when they are followed by a Direct Object

SORTIR (être)	Je suis sorti(e) hier soir. ***(je suee sokhti ehek sua)***	I went out last night.
SORTIR (avoir)	J'ai sorti le lit de ma chambre. ***(jai sokhti le lee de ma shambhr)***	I took the bed out of my room.
DESCENDRE (être)	Je suis descendu(e) dans l'ascenseur. ***(je suee descendu danz lasunsieur)***	I came down in the elevator.
DESCENDRE (avoir)	J'ai descendu le criminel. ***(jai descendu le khreeminal)***	I brought down the criminal.

MONTER (être)	Je suis monté par l'escalier. ***(je suee monte pah lesclayeer)***	I came up by the stairs.
PASSER (être)	Je suis passé par la Tour Eiffel. ***(je suee passé pah la tour ifel)***	I passed by the Eiffel Tower.
PASSER (avoir)	J'ai passé mon examen de maths. ***(jai passé maun exama de maths)***	I took my math test. (NB: to pass an exam is réussir; to take an exam, use passer)

2. Reflexive verbs always take être.

This distinguishes them from verbs with preceding objects pronouns.

Reflexive Verbs vs. Verbs with Preceding Object Pronouns

Je me suis parlé. ***(je me suee pakhle)***	I spoke to myself.
Il m'est parlé. ***(eel may pakhle)***	He spoke to me.
Elle s'est regardé en miroir. ***(el say regardhe on meehor)***	She look herself in the mirror.

Le Leçon 20

Le Future

This tense is used to express what someone will do or will be doing or something that will happen or will be happening:

Je ferai le gateau ce soir. ***(je ferai le gato ce sua)***	I will make cake this evening.
Est-ce que vous passeriez le derniére examen? ***(esk vooz passerez le dehneeyer exama)***	Will you take the final exam?

Future tense of regular verbs

The future tense of regular verbs is formed by adding the endings shown in Table 1

TABLE 1 The Future of Regular Verbs				
Subject	**Ending**	**-er Verbs**	**-ir Verbs**	**-re Verbs**
je	-ai	jouerai	finirai	rendrai
tu	-as	joueras	finiras	rendras
il/elle/on	-a	jouera	finira	rendra
nous	-ons	jouerons	finirons	rendrons
vous	-ez	jouerez	finirez	rendrez
ils/elles/on	-ont	joueront	finiront	rendront

Note that the ending for the je, tu, il, and ils form is the present tense of avoir. The nous form is formed by adding -ons; the vous form is formed by adding -ez.

Note the following about forming the future tense of regular verbs:

- **Endings are added to the complete infinitive of -er and -ir verbs.**
- **For -re verbs, drop the final e before adding the appropriate future ending:**
    - rendre: ils rendront
- **For -er verbs, if the stem has two consecutive pronounced consonants before -er, the e of the -er infinitive ending is pronounced:**
    - parler: il parlera
- **If the stem has one pronounced consonant before -er, the e of the -er infinitive is silent:**
    - diner: nous dînerons

Spelling changes in the future tense

All verbs that require spelling changes form the future in the same way as regular verbs: infinitive + future ending. The following are exceptions to this rule:

- **For verbs ending in -yer (except envoyer, which is irregular and has enverr- as its stem), change y to i in all forms of the future tense. Verbs ending in -ayer may or may not make this change:**
    - je netto ierai, nous netto ierons (I will clean, we will clean)
    - j'essa ierai or j'essa yerai (I will try)
- **For verbs ending in e + consonant + - er (but not é + consonant + -er), change the silent e before the infinitive ending to é in all forms of the future tense:**
    - tu am éneras, vous am énerez (you will bring)
- **With appeler and jeter, double the consonant in the future tense:**

- vous appellerez (you will call)
  (vooz appelray)
- vous jetterez (you will throw)
  (vooz jettray)

Future Tense of Irregular Verbs

Verbs that are irregular in the future (and the derivatives of these verbs) have future stems (verb forms to which endings are added) ending in -r or -rr. Add the future endings to these stems to get the correct future form, as shown in the following list.

Infinitive -Pronunciation	Future Stem
aller (to go) ***alay***	ir-
apercevoir (to notice) ***apercevah***	apercevr-
asseoir (to seat) ***assuar***	assiér- or assoir-
avoir (to have) ***avah***	aur-
courir (to run) ***koureer***	courr-
cueillir (to pick) ***keeyah***	cueiller-
devoir (to have to) ***devah***	devr-
Envoyer (to send) ***onvoyeh***	enverr-
ìtre (to be) ***eth***	ser-
faire (to make, to do) ***feh***	fer-
falloir (to be necessary) ***fallua***	faudr-
mourir (to die) ***mureer***	mourr-

Pleuvoir (to rain) ***plvah***	pleuvr-
pouvoir (to be able to) ***puvah***	pourr-
Recevoir (to receive) ***recvah***	recevr-
savoir (to know) ***savah***	saur-
tenir (to hold) ***teneer***	tiendr-
valoir (to be worth) ***valua***	vaudr-
venir (to come) ***veneeh***	viendr-
voir (to see) ***vua***	verr-
vouloir (to wish, to want) ***vulua***	voudr-

- For example:

n ville cet après-midi.

(jeerahi aveel seth apreh meedee) (I'll go downtown this afternoon.)

- Tu recevras une surprise.
  (tu recevah eun suphreez) (You'll receive a surprise.)

Irregularities in the future a so occur in related verbs:

- Je te reverrai demain.
  (je te revrayee dema) *(I'll see you tomorrow.)*

Negating in the future tense

To negate a sentence in the future, simply put ne and the negative word around the conjugated verb:

- Nous ne saurons pas tout de suite les résultats.
  (nooz ne soro pa tut de suut lez resoolt) (We won't know the results immediately.)

- Il ne fera rien demain.

(ele ne fera rhia dema)	(He won't do anything tomorrow.)

Remember that pronouns remain before the conjugated verb:

- Elle ne t'enverra pas le paquet avant mercredi.

(el ne tonvera pa le packet avo mekhredi)	(She won't send you the package before Wednesday.)

Questions in the future

To form a question using inversion, reverse the order of the subject pronoun and the verb and join them with a hyphen:

- Fera-t-il une partie de tennis ce matin?

(fera til eun pakhti de tennees ce mata)	(Will he play a game of tennis this morning?)

- Travaillerez-vous pendant le week-end?

(thavaiye vooz pondo le weekon)	(Will you work on the weekend?)

To negate an inverted question, put ne and the negative expression around the inverted form. Remember that all object and adverbial pronouns must remain before the conjugated form of the verb:

- Ne lui direz-vous pas la vérité?

(ne luee dhire cooz pa la veheete)	(Won't you tell him [her] the truth?)

- N'y iront-elles pas?

(nee ero el pas)	(Won't they go there?)

Uses of the future

Note the following about when and when not to use the future in French:

- **Be careful to distinguish "will" as used to form the future and the verb vouloir (to wish, to want), which translates as "will" when it expresses "willingness":**

- Je t'aiderai.

  (je tai derae) (I will help you.)

- Veux-tu m'aider?

  (veux tu maidera) (Will you [do you wish, are you willing to] help me?)

- **The future tense is NOT used in French in a subordinate clause requiring the subjunctive:**

- Je doute qu'il réussisse.

  (je dut keel rehusee) (I doubt he will succeed.)

- **When the main clause is in the present tense, the future or the present may be used after croire que (to believe that), penser que (to think that), savoir que (to know that), espérer que (to hope that), and ne pas savoir si (to not know if) to express a future action:**

- Je pense qu'il vient.

  (je paunse keel viya)

- Je pense qu'il viendra.

  (je paunse keel veyendera) I think he is coming (is going to come, will come).

- **The future may be used conversationally to express probability or supposition, especially with avoir and ìtre:**

- Elle ne mange rien. Elle sera malade.

  (el ne maung rhian. (She isn't eating anything.

  El sera malaad) She must be sick.)

- Il crie de toutes ses forces. Il aura peur.

  (eel crhee de tut sez fohs) (He's screaming at the top of his lungs. He must be afraid.)

- **The future tense is used after the following conjunctions of time when the verb in the main clause is in the future tense, even if the present tense is used in English:**

  quand, lorsque, au moment où (when)

- Je lui parlerai quand (lorsque, au moment où) il arrivera.

(je luee pakhlei kaun eel aheevra)	(I will speak to him when he arrives.)

dès que, aussitôt que (as soon as)

- Dès que (Aussitôt que) tu me téléphoneras, je viendrai te chercher.

(dez k tu me telephone, je viendhrai te chekhche)	(As soon as you call me, I'll come find you.)

pendant que, tandis que (while)

- Je lirai pendant que (tandis que) mon mari jouera au golf.

(je leehrai paundo k maun mahee jouera o golf)	(I'll read while my husband is playing golf.)

Le Leçon 21

Future Anterieur

The futur antérieur (future perfect) is used to express a future action or event that will be completed before another future action or to describe a future action or event that will have been completed in the future.

Forming the futur antérieur

The futur antérieur is formed by using the future tense of the helping verb (avoir or itre) + the past participle of the action being performed. The futur antérieur tells what the subject will or shall have done:

- Ils auront fini avant mon départ.

  (eel zoho feenee avo maun deparkht) (They will have finished before my departure.)

- Nous serons déjá partis quand vous arriverez.

  (nooz seho deja pakhtee kaun vooz arheeve) (We will have already left when you arrive.)

- Les enfants se seront déjá couchés quand leurs parents reviendront.

  (Lez onfo se seho deja coushe kaun leurz paho reveyendro) (The children will have already gone to bed when their parents return.)

- Demain á cette heure, il sera revenu de son voyage.

  (dema a set a, eel sera revenu de saun voyage) (Tomorrow at this time, he will have come back from his trip.)

• Negating the futur antérieur

To negate a sentence in the futur antérieur, simply put ne and the negative word around the conjugated helping verb:

- Je n'aurai pas fini mon travail avant minuit.

(je naurai pa feenee thavai minuee)	(I will not have finished my work before midnight.)

- Il n'aura rien accompli.

(eel naura rhian accomplee)	(He will have accomplished nothing.)

Remember that pronouns remain before the conjugated verb:

- Je n'y serai pas allé avant lundi.

(je nee serayee all avo lundee)	(I will not have gone there before Monday.)

Questions in the futur antérieur

To form a question using inversion, reverse the order of the subject pronoun and the verb and join them with a hyphen. Use -t- to link two vowels:

- Sera-t-elle revenue avant la fin de mai?

(sera tel revenue avo la feenee de may)	(Will she have returned before the end of May?)

To negate an inverted question, put ne and the negative expression around the inverted form. Remember that all object and adverbial pronouns must remain before the conjugated form of the verb:

- N'aura-t-il pas fini le travail?

(naura teel pa feenee le thavayee)	(Won't he have finished the work?)

- Ne l'aura-t-il pas fini?

(ne laura teel pa feenee)	(Won't he have finished it?)

Uses of the futur antérieur

The futur antérieur is used after the conjunctions quand (when), lorsque (when), aussitôt que (as soon as), dès que (as soon as), and après que (after) when the future is used in the main clause:

- Après que nos invités seront partis, nous nous coucherons

(aprhe k noz anveete serho pakhtee, nooz nooz coshero)	(As soon as our guests have left, we will go to bed.)

The futur antérieur is also used to express probability or supposition in the past:

- Il n'est pas venu. Il aura oublié notre rendez-vous.

(eel ne pas venu. Eel aura ublee nothr rendez vooz)	(He didn't come. He must have forgotten our appointment.)

- Elle est en retard. Il sera arrivé quelque chose.

(eel a o rethard. Eel seha arheeve kelkchoze)	(She's late. Something must have happened.)

Le Leçon 22

Plus-que parfait.

The Plus Que Parfait

The plus-que-parfait (the pluperfect) indicates that an action had taken place and had been completed before another past action took place. The plus-que-parfait is the compound form of the imperfect and is formed by using the imperfect of the appropriate helping verb (avoir or être) + the past participle of the verb. Its English equivalent is "had" + past participle:

- J'avais mal á l'estomac parce que j'avais trop mangé.

(javee maal e stomac parck javai thro mange)	(I had a stomachache because I had eaten too much.)

- Il marchait avec peine parce qu'il était tombé.

(eel makhshe avec paan parsk keel ate tombe)	(He walked with difficulty because he had fallen.)

- Elle s'était préparée avant de donner sa présentation.

(eel setait preparc avo de donneh sa presautacion)	(She had prepared herself before giving her presentation.)

Le Leçon 23

Passe anterieur

The passé antérieur is used after conjunctions of time — aussitôt que and dès que (as soon as), quand and lorsque (when), and après que (after) — to show that an action was completed before another action (expressed by the passé simple) took place.

Quand nous eûmes fini, nous mangeâmes.

(kaun nooz eum feenee, nous mangeom)	When we had finished, we ate.

Dès qu'elle fut arrivée, le téléphone sonna.

(dez kel fu arheeve, le telephonme sonna)	As soon as she arrived, the phone rang.

Je partis après que vous fûtes tombé.

(je pakhtee apreh k vooz tut taumbe)	I left after you fell.

Le Leçon 24

Le Feu de signalization
(le fo de signalizaeo)

English	*French*
Traffic	La circulation* ***(la circulacio)***
Road	La route ***(la hoot)***
Motorway	Une autoroute ***(eun autoho**ot)*
Roundabout	Le Rond-point***(le raund puant)***
Zebra crossing	Le passage piétons ***(la passag peeteo)***
Pedestrian	Le piéton ***(le peeteo)***
Driver	Le conducteur(ice) ***(le conducthreece)***
Road cign	Le panneau de signalisation***(la pano de signalizaeo)***
Speed limit	La limitation de vitesse ***(la leemeetacio de veetes)***
Traffic jam	Un bouchon, Un embouteillage***(un bousho, un ombuaiyaz)***
Accident	Un Accident***(un accseedo)***
Traffic light	Le feu de signalisation ***(le fo de signalizaeo)***
One way	Le sens unique***(le sau unik)***
No entry	Le sens interdit ***(le sau anteridit)***
Divertion	La deviation***(la deveeacio)***

Emergency lane	La bande d'arrêt d'urgence ***(la band dahet duhgaunce)***
Pay Toll	Le Péage ***(la page)***
Bridge	Le pont***(le po)***
Overtake	Le dépassement ***(le depassmo)***
Slowdown	Ralentir ***(ralenteeh)***
Break down	Tomber en panne***(tombe o pan)***

Il y a un accident.

(eelya un acceedo) There is an accident.

Ne pas dépassez ou ne dépasse pas..

(ne pa dephasse ou ne dephass pa) Do not overtake.

La limite de vitesse est 90 km.

(la leemeet de veetes a quatre vingt dix) The speed limit is 90 km.

Le rond point est sur la gauche.

(le rhond puant a suh la gosh) The roundabout is on the left.

Left – la gauche ***(la gosh)***

Right – la doigt ***(la duat)***

Hotel Novotel

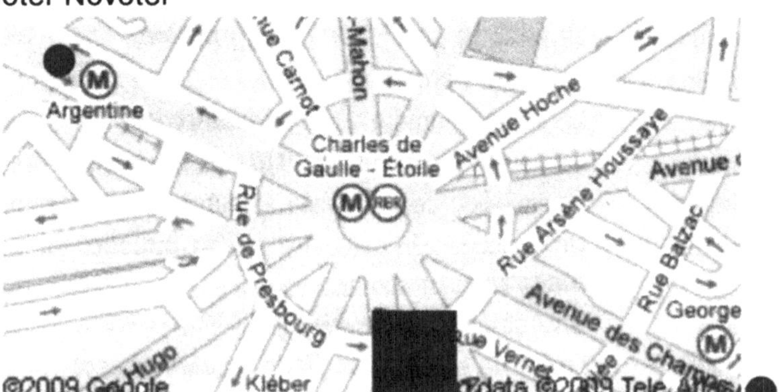

l aérôprt

Le visiteur:Bonjour Monsieur! ***(bonju mauseeur)***

Vous:Bonjour! ***(bonju)***

Le visiteur:Dites moi le direction de aéroport au l'hôtel Novotel, sil vous plait! ***(deet mua le direcio de aehopoht o lotel Novotel, sil vooz play)***

Vous:biensûr!***(beasur)***

Vous:Prenez le route droit, après deux kilometer vous trouverez le passage piétons, ne prenez pas. Vous serez le rue Avenue des Champsé, prenez le meme rue. Finallement vous trouverez le rond point, de lá tournerez gauche, prenez le rue seize et conduirez le route droit. Á le dernier du rue, en gauche il y a l'hôtel Novotel.

(prhone le rooht duat, apreh deux keelometer vooz throuvez le passage peyeto, ne prehene pas. Vooz sereh le ruh avenue dez shamp, prhone le maim ruh. Feenalmo vooz throuvez le rhond puant, de la tourncy gosh, prehone le rhu sez a conduihe le rout duat. A le dehneeyer du ruh, o gosh eelya lotel Novotel.)

Visiteur: Merci mille fois! ***(mehsi meel fua)***

L'exercise description de la photo.

Le Leçon 25

Les nom de robes en français

pants = pantalon (m)***(paantlo)***

skirt = jupe (f)***(jup)***

socks= chaussettes (f/pl)
(shoset)

shoes = chaussure f
(shoser)

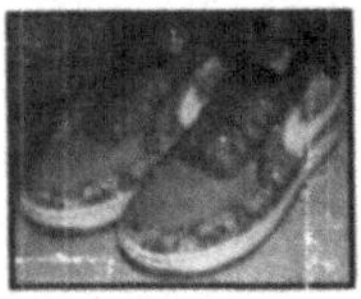

jeans= jean m (singular= où est mon jean?)
(jaun)

scarf= écharpe/foulard f

gloves= gants m/pl

(asharp)

coat= manteau m

(manto)

cap= casquette f

(kasket)

dress= robe f

(rhob)

swim suit= maillot de bain (m)

(maɔeyo de bain)

(gaunt)

panties= sous-vêtements m/pl

(***su-votmo)***

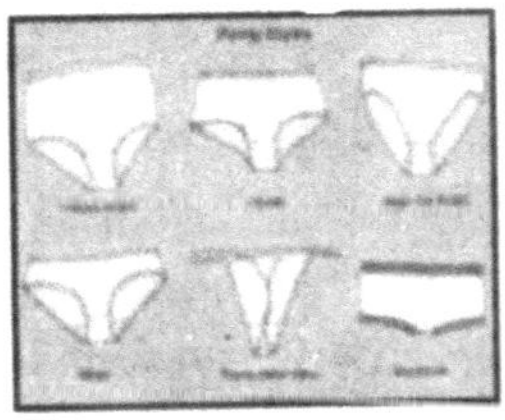

hat=chapeau m

(shapo)

tie=cravatte f

(khravet)

Le Leçon 26

LES COULEURS

English	masc sing.	fem sing.	masc plural	fem plural
Purple	violet	Violette	Violets	Violettes
	(ylet)	*(ylet)*	*(ylet)*	*(ylet)*
Blue	bleu	Bleue	Bleus	Bleues
	(blo)	*(blo)*	*(blo)*	*(blo)*
green	vert	Verte	Verts	Vertes
	(veht)	*(veht)*	*(veht)*	*(veht)*
yellow	jaune	Jaune	Jaunes	Jaunes
	(jaung)	*(jaung)*	*(jaung)*	*(jaung)*
orange	orange	Orange	Orange	Orange
	(ohanj)	*(ohanj)*	*(ohanj)*	*(ohanj)*
red	rouge	Rouge	Rouges	Rouges
	rouz	*Rouz*	*Rouz*	*rouz*
black	noir	Noire	Noirs	Noires
	(nuar)	*(nuar)*	*(nuar)*	*(nuar)*
white	blanc	Blanche	Blancs	Blanches
	(blansh)	*(blansh)*	*(blansh)*	*(blansh)*
grey	gris	Grise	Gris	Grises
	(grees)	*(grees)*	*(grees)*	*(grees)*
brown	marron	Marron	Marron	Marron
	(mahoon)	*(mahoon)*	*(mahoon)*	*(mahoon)*
pink	rose	Rose	Roses	Roses
	(roz)	*(mahoon)*	*(mahoon)*	*(mahoon)*
light blue	bleu clair	bleu clair	bleu clair	bleu clair
	(blo clair)	*(blo clair)*	*(blo clair)*	*(blo clair)*
dark blue	bleu foncé	bleu foncé	bleu foncé	bleu foncé
	(blo fonce)	*(blo fonce)*	*(blo fonce)*	*(blo fonce)*

Examples:

J'ai le verte voiture.
(jai le veht vachyu)

Est ce que tu as le jupe de blanche?
(esk tu a le jup de blansh)

Nous avons le stylo noir.
(nooz zavo le steelo nuar)

le ceil est bleu.
(le cial a blo)

Elle porte le chatêau et le robe rose.
(el pokht la shato a le rohb roz)

Il est mon cravette gris.
(eel a maun chravet ghees)

Une chemise verte clair(light green)
(eun shaumeez veht clair)

Le Déscription de l'personne.

J'ai un ami qui s'appelle John, Il est très gentil, hônet et bon. Il a les cheveux rouge, le visage round et le taille grand. Toute le soir il viens ma maison. J'aime étudie et joue avec lui.Il ya quatre personne dans sa famille, deux frère et deux sœur.

(jai a maee kee sapel John, eel a thre jauntily, oneth a bo. Eel a les chev rouz, le veesaj rondhr ale taeel ghand. Tut le sua el veeya ma maizo. Jaime atudeeye avex luee. Eelya cathr pehson danz sa famille, deux freh a deux sir.)

Le Leçon 27

Faire de ménage

English	**French**
to do the housework	faire le ménage***(feh le menaz)***
to make the bed	faire le lit ***(feh le lee)***
to do the laundry	faire la lessive***(feh la leseev)***
to do the washing	faire la lessive***(feh la leseev)***
to do the ironing	faire le repassage ***(feh le repasaz)***
to do the cooking	faire la cuisine***(feh la kyuseen)***
to prepare a meal	préparer un repas ***(prepare a repa)***
to lay the table	mettre le couvert (***methr le couverht)***
to do the dishes	faire la vaisselle***(feh la vasail)***
to run errands	faire des courses(***feh dez coorse)***
to break	casser***(casse)***
to cut	couper***(kupe)***
to mix	melanger ***(melanze)***

Nom des objets

Il ya deux machine laver.
(eelya doux masheen) There are two washing machine.

La femme debasse les vêtements.
(la farm debhasse lez vetmo) The lady is collecting the clothes.

Il ya serviette.
(eelya sehveeyet) There is a towel.

Elle a lave les vêtements.
(el a laav lez vetmo) She washed the clothes.

Elle porte la robe bleu.
(el pokht la rohb blo) She is wearing blue dress.

Le Leçon 28

Le conversation *(le convehsacio)*

A.Le docteur *(l dokhter)* et la patient *(pahcio)*

P:Hello!	Bonjour! ***(bonju)***
D:Hello! What happened! suffering from fever since yesterday!	Bonjour!Que-ce qu'il y a ***!(kesek keeleeya)*** ***(je suee maalad, jai le fever depuee Eehek)***
D:It seems to be malaria	c'est paraît le malaria.***(se le pahait malereea)***
D: never mind, you will be Alright, I will give you some medicines	n'enqûete pas, je vous aurai conseil les medicaments***(na onket pas, je vooz auraee consei les medicamo)***
P:I couldn't sleep all night I have a pain in the throat	Je ne peux pas dormir toute le nuit. J'ai mal a la gorge.***(je ne p pas Dohmee tut le nuee)(jai mal a la gosh)***
D:I will give you injection.	Je vous donne la injection.***(je vooz daun la anjection)***
P:How much I have to pay You?	Combien je vous paye***?(caumbian je Vooz pay)***
D: Rs 100	Rupee Cent. ***(roopee sau)***
P: Thank you!	Merci ***(mehcee)***

B. Le Frère (l freh) et la fille (fee)

Fille: Goodmorning!	Bonjour papa***!(bonju papa)***
Frère:Goodmorning my Daughter!	Bonjour ma fille***(bonju ma fee)***
Fille:I got up so late.	Je me suis lave plus tard.***(je me suee plu tarhd).***

Frère: no problem, today is Sunday	pas de problem, nous sommes le Dimanche*(pa de problem, nooz zom Le dimaksh)*
Fille:where is mummy?	Où est mama?*(ou a mama)*
Frère: She is in the kitchen, Preparing breakfast.	elle est dans le cuisine, preparer le petite dejeuner.*(el a danz le kyuscene Prepareh le petit dejene)*
Fille:something special.	Quel que chose special. *(kel k shoes speceeal)*
Frère:cake.	Le gateau.*(le gato)*
Fille:Today I am going out With my friends	Aujourd'hui j'irai avec mes amis.*(ojourdhuee jeerai avec mez amee)*
Frère:go-ahead, where Are you going?	vas-y , où le vas?(*vaa zee, oo le va).*
Fille: zoo.	Le zoo.*(le zu)*

C.la mere et le fils ***.(la meh ale fees)***

Mère:hey my son, are You back?	mon fils, tu rentres?*(maun fis, tu ontr)*
Fils:yes, class got cancelled.	Oui, le sale a annulé.*(ouee, le saal a Annule)*
Mère:are you tired?	As tu fatigue*?(aa tu fatige)*
Fils:yes, I played hockey For 2 hrs.	oui, j'ai joué le hockey pour deux heure.*(ouee,jai jouee le ockie pur de he)*
Mère:if you want take bath, In the meanwhile I will prepare tea.	sit u veux me laver, pendat ce temps je prepare le thè.(*see tu veux me lave, Paundant ce taump)*
Fils:ok.	D'accord!(*dahco)*
Mère: keep your clothes in the bathroom, I will wash them later.	mettres votre vêtement dans la salle de bain, je les laverai plustard.*(met vothr Vontmo danz la saal de baa, je les laveree plustarhd)*
File:ok	cava! *(sava)*
Mère:There are the sweets On the table Which has come from Mohan's house.	Il y a les bonbon qui donner par Mohan *(eclcoya lez baunbaon kee donneh Pah Mohan)*
File:Oh I remember his sister got engaged.	Oh, Je souvniens, c'est sa sœur A engage*(je souveeya, ce sa sir aa engage.*

D.Le visit au zoo *(le veeseet o zoo)*

Dilip:Gopal yesterday you were went where?	Gopal, où tu as allé***?(gopal, oo tu aa Allee.)***
Gopal: I went to the zoo.	Je suis allé au zoo.***(je suee allee ou zoo)***
Dilip:alone	seul.***(sel)***
Gopla:yes	oui.***(ouee)***
Dilip:Why did you go Alone, I would have Accompanied you.	puorquoi tu as allé seul, je tu ai accompané.***(pukcoi tu aa alle,jet u a Accompnee)***
Gopal:Next time I will Surely tell you.	prochain, je tu demanderai surememt. ***(prochain, jet u deemanderahi suhmo)***
Dilip: I visited to Bombay Zoo when I was young	j'ai visité au zoo de Bombay quand J'étais plus jeune.***(jai veeseete o zoo De Bombay co jetai plus jung)***
Gopal:This zoo is ver big And you will find all types Of animals here.	ceux zoo est très grand et varieté de animaux ici.***(ce zoo a thre ghand a Vahite de aneemo eecee.)***
Dilip:how did you go?	Comment as tu allé? ***(kamo as tu alle?)***
Gopal: I took the bus, I got down near to the Zoo, there was the long Queue to purchase tickets.	J'ai pris le autobus, je suis descendu prés au zoo, le queue étais trop longue acheter le billet.***(jai pree le otobus, je Suee ete thro long acheete le beeyee)***
Dilip: what type of animals Have you seen?	quells types des animaux tu as vu? ***(kel teep dez aneemo tu aa voo)***
Gopal: there are tigers, Rhinoceros, deer, monkey	il y sont le tigre, le rhinocéros, le singe ***(eel so le teegr, le rhocero, le sanj)***

E.Dans le salle

Etudiante(*atudeeyant*) et le Professeur*(profehsir)*

E: Good morning sir!	Bonjour***(bonju)***
P:Good morning students!	Bonjour étudiants***(bonju atudeeyants)***
E: Sir, it has been raining Heavenly since early morning.	Sir, c'est le pluie depuis tôt le matin ***(sir, ce le pluee depuee tot le mata)***
P: Have you all done your	sommes nous faire le travail?

Homework?	***(som nooz fair le thavai)***
E: Yes sir.	Oui.
P: I will ask some of the Questions on general Knowledge.	Je vous demande quelque questions du culture général.***(je vooz demand Kel ke keschio doo culture genhal)***
E:please ask easy questions.	Demandez questions simple sil vous plâit.***(demaand keschio sampl sil vooz play)***.
P:sure, who was the first of India.	sûre, qui étais le prime minister Prime minister prémier***?(sur, kee ate le preeme meeneestr prohmier)***
E: Pt Jawahar lal Nehru	Pt Jawahar lal Nehru
P: When India became Independent?	quand Inde a devenue indépendant ? En quel année***(kau and a devenu andepaunde?***
E: in 1947.	en mille neuf cent quatre sept. ***(o meel nef sau cathr set)***
P:what is museum?	Quel le musée?***(kel le muze)***
E: The place where Historical things are kept.	le place où les choses historique a mis. ***(le plas ou les shose istorik a mee)***
P:last question. How many Colours are in rainbow?	dernier question. Combien les couleurs en arc de ciel?(***dehneer Kesschio.Combeean les couler on ark de ceal?***
E: seven colours.	Sept couleurs.***(seth koolerz)***

F.Demander le route *(demandeh le ruut)*

Étranger et le visiteur. *(atranje a le veeseeter)*

V:excuse me. I am new At this place.	Excusez moi!Je suis Étranger ici.***(xcuse mua! je suee atrange ici)***
E:no problem. How can I help you!	Pas de problem! Je vous aide***?*** ***(pa de problem!je vooz Aid)***
V:Can you please tell me how to Reach to Sarita Vihar.	pouvez vous me direz, comment arriver au Sarita Vihar.***(puve vooz Me deeh commo arheeve o sarita vihar)***

E:ofcoursetake this road, leave first Right and take second right. Afer Teo kilometer you will find the roundabout, just after that sarita vihar starts.	Biensûr!prenez le cette rue Laissez premiére doit et prenez le Doit deuxiéme. Aprés deux kilometer Vous trouvez le rond point, juste Après ça, sarita vihar Commences. ***(beeya sur!prohne le cet ruu,laise prohmeeye duat a prohne le duat dxieme. Aprhe de kilmeehtr vooz throuve le rhond puant, juste aprhe sa, sarita vihar commence.)***
V:Thanks you!	merci! ***(mehcee)***

Le Leçon 29

Les phrases des quotiendien ***(lez faz dez kutodeeon)***

Day to day phrases

Hello	Bon'jour***(bonju)***
Happy New Year	Bonne année***(baun anne)***
Same to you!	Meme vous***(mem vooz)***
Happy Birthday!	Bon anniversaire***(baun anneeverseh)***
Welcome you all!	Bienvenu***(beeavenu)***
Congratulations!	Felicitations***(feleeceetacion)***
Thanks for your visit!	Merci pour votre visite***(mehci pu vothr veesit)***
My god!	Mon dieu!***(maun diu)***
Oh my darling!	Mon chouchou***(maun shushu)***
Bravo!	Bravo***(brahvo)***
Excellent!	Excellent***(xseelont)***
How terrible!	Terrible ça***(tehreeble sa0***
How beautiful!	Belle!***(bel)***
Really	réelement(***realmo)***
Certainly!	Certainment!***(certehnmo)***
With best compliments!	Amitié***(ameeteeye)***
Just a minute!	Juste a minute!***(juust a meenuet)***
Any more!	Plus!***(pluus)***
Enough!	Assez***(assee)***
Anything else!	Quelque chose!
No worry!	Pas ênquiete!***(pa onkeeyet)***
As you like!	Faire vous veulent!***(teh vooz vel)***
Not at all!	Pas du tout!***(pa du tut)***
For ladies	pour femmes***(pur farm)***

No admission	interdit***(ntredheet)***
No talking!	Ne parlez pas***(ne pakhle pa)***
No smoking	pas fumez ***(pa fume)***
No parking!	Defense de stationer***(deefonse de sthacione)***
No exit!	Pas sortie***!(pa sohtee)***
Be quick!	Rapid(***rhapeed)***
Come in !	vien sil vous plait!***(veeya sil vooz play)***
Don't talk rot!	Ne parlez mal!***(ne pakh maal)***
Be careful!	Prudemment ***(proodmo)***
Speak the truth!	Parler le vérité***!(parkhle le veheete)***

Le Leçon 30

Les questions

Is the ḥindi difficult	Est-ce que l'hindi difficult? ***(esk leendi deefeecult)***
are you afraid of ghost?	Vous êtes peur de fantôme? ***(Vooz zet per de fatome)***
Am I a fool?	Je suis stupid? ***(Je suee stupeed)***
Was the moon shining?	La lune brillait-il ? ***(La loon brheetaee-il)***
why are you so sad?	Pourquoi tu as triste? ***Pukua tu a thrist?***
Why does he didn't Try for this post?	pouquoi il n'essaye pas Pour cet poste? ***(pukua eel na essay pas pur cet post)***
Did you understand	avez vous compris? ***(ave vooz comprhi)***
do you like travelling abroad?	Vous aimez voyger l'étranger? ***(vooz aime voyage 'etranger)***
she is having a headache?	Elle a mal a la tête? ***(L a maal a la tet)***
aren't you going to office?	Êtes vous aller au bureau? ***(eth vooz alle o buro)***
has he come for some important work?	est ce que il viens pour le travail Important? ***(esk eel viya pur le thavai impokhtant)***
May I give you the advice?	Peux je vous conseil? ***(p je vooz consaee)***

Who lives here?	Qui habite ici? ***(Kee abet ici)***
do you prefer tea or coffee?	Est-ce que vous preferez le thè ou le café? ***(esk vooz prefere le the ou le café)***
is it impossible?	C'est le impossible? ***(ce le imposseebl)***
are you it is certain?	Êtes vous c'est certain? ***(Eth vooz cest certain)***
she likes household work?	Elle aime le faire de ménage? ***(el aime le faire de ménage)***
which is your favourite book?	Quel livre tu es favourite? ***(kel leevr tu as favoreet)***
are you opening the window?	Êtes vous ouvre le fenêtre? ***(eth vooz ouvre le feneth)***
you didn't bring the umbrella?	Tu n'apporte pas le parapluie? ***(tu n'apporte pa le parapluee)***

Le leçon 31

les phrases

I want to buy the dress?	Je veux acheter les chausseurs ***(je veux acheete le chaussers)***
Is the shirt ready?	Est le chemise prêt? ***(a le chaumeez preth)***
I must get these clothes Within this week.	Je dois les vetêments dans cette Semaine***(je dua lez votmo danz cet semen)***
I am very happy	Je suis très content. ***(je suee thre conto)***
How is your father?	Comment est ton papa? ***(commo a taun papa)***
I am very angry	Je suis en colére. ***(je suee o coler)***
he is better than yesterday.	Il est très bien comme hier. ***(eel a thre bean com ehek)***
I have a toothache.	Je suis mal en dent. ***(je suee maal o daun)***
I like red vine.	J'aime le vin rouge. ***(jame le va rouz)***
she is very tired	elle est fatigue/ ***(el a fateeg)***
they are sleeping.	Ils dormant. ***(eel dormho)***
Do you understand English?	Est-ce que vous comprenez anglais? ***(esk vooz comprenc onglc)***
I am going by TGV.	je vais en TGV. ***(je vae o TEZEEVEE)***

I don't have money for Purchasing pen.	je n'ai pas le monnaie acheter le stylo. ***(je ne pas le mona cshete le steelo)***
Are you watching the News channel?	est-ce que vous regardez le châine de Nouvelle? ***(esk vooz regardez le shane de novel)***
I like watching cartoon Channel.	J'aime regardez le châine de bande Dessiné ***(jame regarde le shane de bond deseene)***

Le leçon 32

Les Comprehensions de la France au AnglaisLucie en France

French- le para une

Lucie, étudiante des États-Unis, vient d'arriver á Charles de Gaulle, l'aéroport qui accueille chaque jour á Paris, 1 million de visiteurs. Paris. Enfin. Ça a toujours été le rêve de Lucie : vivre dans la Ville lumière, la ville des beaux arts, du quartier latin, du vin, et qui sait, peut-être la ville d'une petite histoire d'amour.

(lucie, atudiant dez etazuni, veeyan dareevay a sharles de gal, lehport kee akkeyee jou a pahi, eun million de veeseeter. Pahi. Onfa, sa a toujou atay le reveh de luci:vivr danz la veel lumeeyeh, la veel dez bo aht, du kehteear latin, du va, a kee say, p athr la veel deun petit istwar damour)

English-Para 1

Lucie, a student from the United States, has just arrived at Charles de Gaulle in Paris, the airport that greets a million visitors to Paris every day. Paris. Finally. It's always been a dream of Lucie's: to live in the City of Light, the city of fine arts, of the Latin Quarter, of wine, and, who knows, perhaps the city of a little love story.

French – le para deux

Son projet est d'étudier en France pendant un an, pour obtenir sa licence dès informatique á l'Université de Versailles á St. Quentin-en-Yvelines. C'est l'université qui lui a offert une bourse pour faire ses études. En plus, sa copine Josephine fait ses études lá-bas, et Lucie va pouvoir vivre avec elle dans son petit appartement.

(saun projay a datudeeye afonce paundo a a , pur obteneeh lisaunce dez informatik a lunivehsitay de versaill a St Quontee o veyen.Say lunivehsitay kee luee offret eun bouhse our feh sez atud. O plus, sa

copeen Jesefeen feh sez atyud la bha, a luci va puvha vivr avec el danz saun petit apakhtmo)

English- Para 2

She plans to study in France for one year, to get her degree in Computer Science at the University of Versailles St. Quentin-en-Yvelines. It's the university that offered her a scholarship to study. Plus, her friend Josephine studies there and Lucie can live with her in a small apartment.

French – Le para throis

Elle prend le RER qui la mène directement á la Gare St. Lazare, en centre-ville. Une fois y arrivée, elle cherche le quai du train pour Versailles. Elle monte dans le train, et bientôt il entre dans un tunnel sombre en direction de Versailles. Lucie est un peu déçue, parce qu'elle doit rester á Versailles bien qu'elle veuille vivre á Paris. Mais elle se dit que Versailles n'est qu'á quelques minutes en train de la grande ville de Paris, et qu'il y a aussi plusieurs attractions á Versailles.

(el prohnd le RER kee la men dheerectmo a la Gah St. Lazah o contr veel. Eun fua e areeheve , el sheshay le kay du tha pur vehsaeel. El motr andz le tha, a bhianto eel ontr danz a tunnel sombhr on dheerecio de vehsail. Luci a ump decu, parck kel duat resther a vehsaeel bea kel vail vevr a pahi. May el se dit k vehsail nay ko kelk mineeut o tha de la ghand veel de pahi, a keelya osi plusiar attracio a vehsaeel.)

English – Para 3

She takes the RER which brings her straight to the St. Lazare station at the city center. After arriving there, she looks for the platform that will take her to the train for Versailles. She boards the train, and soon it's heading into a black tunnel toward Versailles. Lucie is a little disappointed because she has to stay in Versailles when she'd like to live in Paris. But she tells herself that Versailles is only a few minutes by train from the big city of Paris, and moreover, there are several attractions in Versailles.

French- Le para quatre

Le train sort du tunnel, et en passant par la grande ville, elle voit un grand cimetière, la tour Eiffel et Montmarte avec la basilique du Sacré-Coeur tout près. Quelques instants plus tard, elle arrive en gare de Versailles.

(le tha sokht doo tunnel, a o passo pah la ghand veel, el vua a ghand ceemeeteeyer, la tur afeel a Montmakht avec la baseeleek du sacre-ker tut preh. Kelk instant plus tahd, el areeheeve o gah de vehsaeel.)

English – Para 4

The train exits the tunnel, and while passing the big city she sees a large cemetery, the Eiffel Tower, and Montmartre with the Sacré Coeur cathedral nearby. A few moments later she arrives at Versailles station.

French- Le para cinq

Elle est arrivée á destination. Devant elle le grand Château de Versailles où Louis XIV, le Roi Soleil, organisa ses fêtes et vécut la grande vie entouré de ses maîtresses. Á droite se trouve l'avenue de St.-Cloud, où est situé l'appartement dans lequel elle va vivre avec Josephine. Fatiguée, mais joyeuse, elle commence á chercher l'adresse de l'appartement. "Toute seule dans un nouveau pays, ne connaissant personne, l'avenir, je t'embrasse vivement ! " se dit Lucie.

(el a areeheeve a destinacio. Devo el la ghand shato de vehsaeel ou louis XIV, le rua solee, orghneeza sez feth a vecu la ghand vea ontournay de sez maithress. A duat se thruv lavenu de St Clo, ou a situay lappakhtmo danz leekel el va vivr avec Josefeen. Fatigay, may jouyes, el kmaunce a shekhshe laddress de lapakhtmo "Tut sul danz a nouvo payz, ne koonaso pehson, laveneer, je taumbhas veevmo! Se dit lucee)

English- Para 5

This is her destination. In front of her is the grand château of Versailles where Louis 14th, the Sun King, had parties and lived the high life with his mistresses. To the right is the avenue St. Cloud where the apartment that she'll live in with Josephine is. Tired, but joyful, she starts looking for the address of the apartment. "All alone in a new country, knowing no one, future, I'm ready!" Lucie says to herself.

Les questions en vrai ou non:

1. Lucie est américaine.
   (lucee a ameerican)
2. Elle est á Paris avec ses parents.
   (el a a Pahee avec sez paho)

3. Elle a déjá un petit ami.

   (el a deja a petit amee)

4. Lucie sera en France pendant deux ans.

   (lucee sera o Fonce pando deux o)

5. Lucie doit payer beaucoup pour ses études.

   (lucee duat payeh boucu pur sez etudeeye)

6. Josephine adore l'informatique.

   (Josefeen adhore laformatik)

7. Lucie préfère habiter á Versailles.

   (lucee prefreh abitay a vehsaeel)

8. Il y aura des choses intéressantes á voir á Versailles.

   (eelya aura dez choz anthreso a vua a vehsaeel)

9. Lucie va vivre seule.

   (lucee va veevr sel)

10. Lucie connaît beaucoup de gens en France.

    (lucee kunaith bucou de gen o fonce.)

Answers:

1)V 2)F 3)F 4)F 5)F 6)F 7)F 8)V

9)F 10)F

Les couleurs de la guerre

French – le para une

Montréal reçoit cet automne une exposition unique au Marché Bonsecours. *Les couleurs de la Guerre* sont des Oeuvres de soldats belges au Front de la Première guerre mondiale (1914-1918).Cette exposition est intéressante par son point de vue historique. En effet, l'on considère souvent les soldats de cette guerre comme des journalistes de leur temps. Il faut dire que la guerre de 1914-18 était moins rapide que celle qui l'a suivie et que ces soldats avaient un peu de répit entre les escarmouches pour dessiner ou peindre les couleurs des saisons. Ainsi, cette exposition nous montre, entre certaines images désolantes de destruction, des paysages pittoresques datant du début du siècle.

(Montreal recua cet autom eun expozicio uneek o Markshay Bonsecurs. Lez coulerz de la gueh so dez ouvrer de soldaat belge o font de la prhomeeyer gueh mondeeal(1914-1918). Cet expozicio a anthreso pah so puant de vu istoreeq. O onfet, lo kaunseedeear souvo lez soldat de cet gueh kaum dez journalist de ler taump. Eel feh deeh k la gueh de 1914-18 etat mua rapheed k cel kee la sueevee a k cez soldat avo ump de repee ontr lez skahmush pur dessene ou pandre lez koulerz dez sayzo. Ainsee cet expozicio nooz montr, ontr cekhtain imag desolant de distrucio, dez paysaz pittoresk dato du debu du seekel)

English- Para 1

Montreal receives this unique autumn exhibition at the Market Bonsecours. The colors of the War are the works of Belgian soldiers to the Forehead of the First World War (1914-1918).This exhibition is interesting by his point of historic view. In fact, one considers often the soldiers of this war as journalists of their time. It is necessary to say that the war of 1914-18 was iess quick than the one that followed it and that these soldiers a little respite between skirmish them to draw or paint the season colors. Thus, this exhibition shows us, between certain distressing pictures of destruction, picturesque landscapes dating back to the century beginning. Also this exhibition is to show the images of the destruction..

French- Le para deux

En effet, l'on y retrouve des représentations des mouvements post-impressioniste, expressioniste, fauviste et cubiste. Les couleurs sont souvent même presque joyeuses.C'est la toute première fois que ces tableaux sont vus de ce côté de l'Atlantique. Ils sont prêtés par le Musée Royal des Armées de Bruxelles dont le curateur était présent parmi les quelque 380 dignitaires présents á l'inauguration pour nous en expliquer les détails.Cette exposition a été organisée par le Consulat général de Belgique á Montréal, le Ministère belge des affaires étrangères et le Musée royal de l'Armée de Bruxelles, avec la participation de la Ville de Montréal.L'exposition se tiendra du 23 octobre au 10 décembre 2000, tous les jours de 10h á 18h.

(on effet, lo e rethrouve dez represontacio dez mouvmo post imprecionist, exprescionist, foveest a cubeest. Lez kolerz so souvo mem presk joyes. Say la tut prohmeeye fua k cez tablo so vu de ce kot de latantik. Eelzo prhet pa le muzay Royal dez Arhmee de Bruxel do le curhater etat prayzo parhmi lez kelk 380 digniteh preayzont a leenoguracio pur nooz o expleek les detail. Cet expozicio a atay orghanize pah le consult genehal de belgik a Montreal, le meeneestar belg dez afair atrongeh a le muzay royal de lahmay de bruxel, avec la participacio de la veel de Montreal. Lexpozicio s teandra du 23 Octobh o 10 Deesaumbh 2000, tus lex jou de 10h a 18h.)

English- Para two

In fact, they have rediscovered representations of the movements of post-impressioniste, expressioniste, fauviste and cubist. The colors are often even almost joyous.It is always the first time that these pictures are seen of this side of the Atlantic. They are lent by the Royal Museum of the Armies of Brussels of which the guardian was present among the some 380 present dignitaries to the inauguration for us to explain the détails.This exhibition was organized by the general Consulate of Belgium to Montreal, the Belgian Ministry of the foreign affairs and the royal Museum of the Army of Brussels, with the participation of the City of Montréal.This exhibition will be held from 23rd October to 10th December 2000, everyday from 10h to 18h.

L'ADMISSION EST GRATUITE- The admission is free.

(ladmscasio a ghachuee)

Les questions en vrai ou non:

1. L'exposition se tiendra en Belgique..

   (lexposeecio sa teendra o belgeek)

2. Ce sont des journalistes qui ont fait les peintures.

   (c so dez journalist kee o feh les pentr)

3. Les peintures ont été faites pendant la guerre.

(les pentr o ate feht pundo la gueh)

4. Toutes les images sont tristes.

   (tut les image so thrist)

5. Il y a une grande variété de styles de peinture.

   (eelya eub gjabd vareehete de steel de pant)

6. Cette exposition a déjá été montrée aux Etats-Unis.

   (cet exposicio a deja ate montre o etazuni)

7. Les tableaux ont été donné au Canada en tant que cadeau.

   (les tablo o ate donay o canada o tant k cado)

8. Le curateur n'a pas assisté á l'inauguration.

   (le cuhater na pa assete a lonoguracio)

9. L'exposition est déjá finie.

   (lexposicio a deja feenee)

11. Il faut payer pour voir l'exposition.

   (el go payeh pur vua lexposicio)

Answers:

1) F 2)F 3)V 4)F 5)V 6)F 7)F 8)F

9)V 10)F

Les lieux de travail sans fume*(lez leey de thavai so fume)*

French- Le para une

Le problème du tabagisme est ignoré d'une bonne partie du monde, alors qu'il est chaudement débattu en Amérique du Nord, plus au Canada qu'aux États-Un d'ailleurs. Les visiteurs venant de pays où fumer du tabac fait encore partie de la norme sociale peuvent trouver étrange que la majorité des

Canadiens (70% dans une étude réalisée par une compagnie canadienne de tabac) ne fume pas et que beaucoup d'autres veuillent arrêter.La province de Colombie britannique vient de franchir une étape supplémentaire. Le Workers' Compensation Board vient de décréter que le tabagisme passif est un danger pour les personnes travaillant dans des lieux où l'on fume. Fumer vient donc d'être interdit par la loi depuis le 1er janvier 2000 dans n'importe quel lieu de travail.

(le problem du tabagism a ignohay dune bon pakhtee du mond, aloh keel a shadmo debattu o Ameerik du nohd, plus o Canada ko Eta u daiyeh. Les veeseeter veno d payz ou fumeh du tabac feh oncor pakhtee de la nohm scial peuv throuveh etronj k la majoreetay dez candaeeyan(70 puhsont danz eun atyud realize pah eun compagnee candaeeyan de tabac) ne fume pa a k boucou dothr vaillaynt areehetay. La proveens de colmobee breetaneek veeya de fransheer eun etap suppleemontairh. Le workers compensacio board veeya de secreter k la tabagism passif a u dangeh pur lez pehson thavaiyya danz dez le ou lao fume . Fuemh veeya donk dethr anthrdit pah la lua depuee le prohmeeyer jaunveeyerdeux meel danz impokht k lieu de thavail.)

English- Para one

The problem of the tobacco use is been unaware of of a good party of the world, while it hotly is debated in North America, more to the Canada than to the one of the States besides. The visitors coming from country where to smoke tobacco still causes left the social norm can find strange that the majority of the Canadians (70% in a study realized by a Canadian company of tobacco) does not smoke and that a lot of others want arrêter.La province of British Colombia has just crossed an additional step. The Workers' Compensation Board has just decreed that the passive tobacco use is a danger for the persons working in places where one smokes. Smoke comes therefore of be forbidden by the law since the 1st January 2000 in any place of work.

French – le para deux

En pratique, vous ne serez donc pas autorisé á fumer du tabac (cigares, pipes, cigarettes) dans tout endroit où travaillent des personnes. Cette nouvelle interdiction comprend tous les endroits où fumer était déjá exclu ainsi que d'autres où c'était encore possible. Les employeurs peuvent construire des pièces distinctes avec des systèmes spéciaux de ventilation approuvés par le Workers' Compensation Board où l'on pourra fumer en toute tranquillité. Cependant, les employés non-fumeurs n'auront l'autorisation de pénétrer dans ces pièces qu'en cas d'urgence.

(o prateek, vooz ne seray donk pa authoreezay afumay du tabac(seegah, peep, seegharet) danz tut onduat ou thavaiyo dez pehson. Cet nouvel anterdicsio comphond tus lez onduat ou funay atat deja xclu ainsi k dauthr, ou saytat oncore possible. Lez omployer puv consthruee dez piyas distinct avec dez sistam specio de venteelacio approvay pah le workers compensacio board ou lon pura fumeh o tut trankeeleetay. Cepaundo danz cez peyes kaun cas duhjaunce.)

English-para two

In practice, you will not be therefore authorized to smoke tobacco (cigars, pipes, cigarettes) in all place where work persons. This new ban understands all the places where to already smoke was excluded as well as of others where it was again possible. The employers can construct distinct pieces with special systems of airiness approved by the Workers' Compensation Board where one will be able to smoke in all quietness. Nevertheless, the employees non-smokers will not have the authorization to penetrate in these pieces that in case of urgency.

French- Le para trios

Les travailleurs de Colombie britannique. Quel effet aura cette nouvelle réglementation sur les personnes cherchant du travail en Colombie britannique?D'après le Workers' Compensation Board, les employés ne seront dorénavant plus obligés de travailler dans un endroit enfumé. Conséquence directe : la diminution potentielle des cancers provoqués par le tabagisme passif. Les personnes souffrant de maladies respiratoires pourront postuler à des fonctions qui leur étaient interdites pour raison de santé.

(lez thavaiyo de colombie breetanik. Kel effet aura cet nouvel reglamacio suh lez pehson shersho du thavai o colombie britaneek / Dhapray le workers compensacio borad, lez omploye ne seroh dorenavo plus obligay de thavaiye danz un onduat ofumay. Consequence dheehect: la diminucio potencial dez cancers provoke pah le tabagism passif. Les pehson soufho de maladee respeehatuar

pouro postulay a dez fonkcio kee ler etaint anterdheet pur raizo de sauntay.)

English-Para three

The workers of British Colombia. Which effect will have this new regulation on the persons looking for of the work in British Colombia? D' after the Workers' Compensation Board, the employees not from now on more will be obliged to work in one smoke out place. Direct consequence: the decrease potentielle of the cancers provoked by the passive tobacco use. The persons suffering from respiratory diseases will be able to apply to functions that were forbidden for them for health reason.

French-Le para quatre

Du point de vue des employeurs, notamment dans les secteurs de l'hôtellerie et de la restauration, cette nouvelle loi va engendrer le licenciement d'une partie de leur personnel et la mise á l'écart de leurs clients fumeurs. Cela pourra prendre des mois avant de voir si les non-fumeurs vont remplacer la clientèle de fumeurs dans tous les bars, les discothèques, les restaurants et les salles de bingo de la province. De nombreux petits établissements craignent de ne pas survivre au changement.

(du puant voo dez employers, notamo danz lez sectors de loteelerier a de la restracio, cet noowell lua va ongendrer le lisensemo deun paklhtee de ler pehsonnel a la meez a lecart de lers cleont fumer. Sela pura prhondr dez mua avo de vua see lez non-fumeh vo raumplsay la cleeontel de fumeh danz tut lez bars, les discothek, les restaurant a lez saal de beenjo de la prohovince. De maumbhes petit etablismo craighno de ne pa suhvive o chanjmo

English- para three

From the point of employers, notably in the sectors of the hôtellerie and restoration, this new law will generate the dismissal on one hand of their personnel and the placement at the gap of their smoking customers. That will be able to take months before seeing if the non-smokers will replace the smoking clients in all the bars, the discos, the restaurants and the bingo halls of the province. Many small establishments are afraid of not to survive the change.

French- Le para cinq

Les employés dans les secteurs de l'hôtellerie et de la restauration attendent anxieusement de voir ce qu'il va se passer quant au nombre de clients, les sommes qu'ils dépenseront et les pourboires qu'ils laisseront. Sur la première semaine de janvier, des restaurants et des pubs auraient été contraints de licencier du personnel, leurs bénéfices ayant subi une baisse de 1.000 $ l'espace d'une semaine suite á la chute de leurs chiffres d'affaires.

(lez omplya danz les secter de lotellier a de la restaracio attondo anziusmo de vua ce kil va se passeh ko o nombhr de cleeont, lez zom kils depsunsero a lez puhbua kil laiseero . Suh la prohmeeyer seemen de jaunvier,dez restaurant a des pub auray atay constraint de lisoncier du pehsonnel, ler beneficier ayay subi eun baisse de 1.000 $ lespass dun seemain duite a la shute de lerz shiffre daffairs.)

English- Para five

The employees in the sectors of the hôtellerie and restoration await anxiously to see what it will happen as for the number of customers, let us are them that they will spend and the tips that they will leave. On the first week of January, restaurants and pubs would have been constrained to dismiss personnel, their profits having undergone a decrease of 1,000 $ the space of a week after the fall of their sales.

Le leçon 33

Le Proverbs

French proverbs offer insight into French culture, history, and society, and are often used in speech and writing. There is no substitute for knowing them, and if you can use them in yourself, so much the better. Below are all the standard proverbs used in French, along with English translations and explanations.

á bon chat, bon rat – ***(a bo shat, bo hath)***
Meaning: tit for tat.

á cœur vaillant rien d'impossible- ***(a kur vaiya rhian dampossible)***
nothing is impossible for a willing heart

á quelque chose malheur est bon***(a kelk shoes malhar a bo)***
for something bad there is good;

aide-toi, le ciel t-aidera ***(aid tua, le ceal tadera)***
God helps those who help themselves

après la pluie, le beau temps***(apreh la pluee, le bo taum)***
good and bad things come one after the other

bien faire et laisser dire***(bean feh a lesse dhih)***
do the work well and let them say what they will

c'est á l'œuvre qu'on connaît l'œuvrier***(say a lovr kaun connaith lauverier)***
a man is judged or known by his works, by the work he does

ce qui est fait n'est plus á faire ***(c kee a feh neh pluz a feh)***
don't leave till tomorrow what can be done today

comparaison n'est pas raison*(compareeson nest pa raizon)*
a comparison proves nothing

de deux maux, il fault choisir le moindre

(de deux ma, eel fo shuazeer le muandr)
choose the lesser of two evils (lit.: given two evils, one must choose the lesser)

deux avis valent mieux qu'un*(deuz avees valo meyer kaun)*
two opinions are worth more than one

donner un œuf pour avoir un bœuf*(doneh un ef pur avah un buf)*
give a little to get a lot

goutte a goutte, l'eau use la Pierre*(goot a goot, lo oos la pcch)*
time and patience yield results.

il faut casser le noyau pour avoir l'amande*(eel fo casseh le noyo pur avah lamand)*
no pain, no gain

il ne faut jamais jeter le manche après la cognée*(eel ne fo jamai jeter le maansh apreh la congee)*
don't give up so easily

il y a un temps pour tout*(eel ya a taump pur tut)*
there is a right time for everything

l'argent n'a pas d'odeur*(largjo na pa dor)*
money has no smell

l'argent ne fait pas le bonheur*(largjo no foh pas le bonhr)*
money can't buy happiness

la parole est d'argent, mais le silence est d'or*(la pahol a dargjo, mein le seelonce a dor)*
words are silver, yet silence is golden

le temps c'est de l'argent*(le taum cest de largJo)*
time is money

les grands esprits se rencontrent***(lez ghond aspire se recontreo)***
great minds think alike

mieux vaut tard que jamais***(meeyeh vo tarhd k jamai)***
better late than never

pas de plaisir sans peine***(pa de plazir saun paan)***
no pleasure without pain

point de nouvelles, bonnes nouvelles***(puant de nuvel, baun nuvel)***
no news is good news

rien ne sert de courir il faut partir a point***(rheen ne soh de cureer eel fo parkhteer a puant)***
nothing is served by running; one must leave at the right time

Rome ne s'est pas fait en un jour***(raum ne eay pas feh a jur)***
Rome wasn't built in a day

tout ce qui brille n'est pas or***(tut ce kee bhee ne pa or)***
all that glitters is not gold

tout est bien qui finit bien***(tut a bean kee finee beean)***
all's well that ends well

vouloir, c'est pouvoir***(vulva, cest puvvah)***
where there's a will, there's a way

Match A with B:

A	B
(a)Le ouvre bouteille ***(le oovr buteii)***	*i)* 
(b) La boule ***(la bool)***	*ii)* 
(c) La infirmière ***(la anfehmeeyer)***	*iii)* 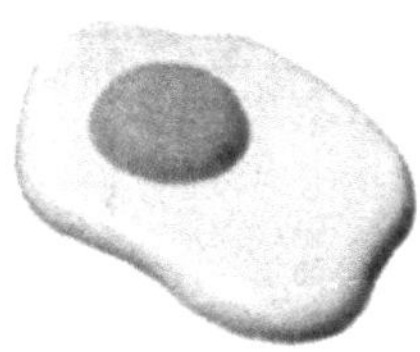
(d) Le calendrier ***(le calndeeyr)***	*iv)* 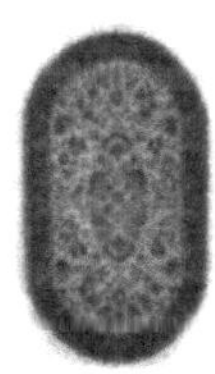
(e) La tapis ***(le tapees)***	*v)* 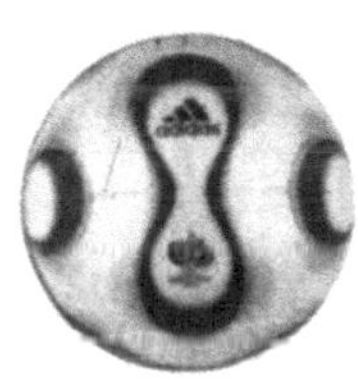

(f) La machine á laver ***(la masheene a lave)***	*vi)* 
(g) La poubelle ***(la pubell)***	*vii)* 
(h) L'œuf ***(lof)***	*viii)* 
(i) La boite ***(la buat)***	*ix)* 
(j) Le beurre ***(la ber)***	*x)* 

Answers:

(a) viii, (b) v, (c) ix, (d) vii, (ẹ) iv, (f) x, (g) i, (h) iii, (i) vi, (j) ii

Le leçon 34

Les Synonyms

Check the meanings in dictionary to understand the formation of the words

1) acquérir*(akeeyeh)* -acheter *(asheetay)*
2) aller*(allay)* -trajet *(thrajay)*
3) Asseoir *(assuar)* - placer*(plasay)*
4) Connaître *(kuneth)* - savoir *(savah)*
5) Courir *(kureer)* - trotter *(trother)*
6) Boire *(buar)* - Absorber*(absorbeh)*
7) Croire*(kuar)* - Présumer *(presumeh)*
8) Dire *(deeh)* -Communiquer *(kamyuneekay)*
9) Dormir *(dohmee)* - Reposer*(repozay)*
10) Essuyer *(asyuyeh)* - Éponger *(apaunjay)*
11) Écrire *(akreeh)* -Calligraphier*(kellygraphy)*
12) Faire*(freh)* - Fabriquer*(fahbreekay)*
13) Finir *(feeneer)* - Termineri**(Tehminay)**
14) Goûter *(goutay)* - Savourer*(savoureh)*
15) Habiter *(abitay)* - Vivre*(veevr)*
16) Joindre *(juandr)* - Connecter*(kooncckth)*
17) Lire *(leeh)* - Déchiffrer*(daysheefrer)*
18) Mentir *(maunteer)* -Désinformer*(dezinformeh)*
19) Mettre *(methr)* - poser *(pozeh)*
20) Mourir *(murir)* - Expirer *(xpoerer)*
21) Naître *(naithr)* - Apparaitre *(appehhtr)*
22) Offrir *(ofreer)* - procurer*(procurer)*

23)	Parler ***(pakhlay)***	- Bavarder***(bavarday)***
24)	Partir ***(pakhteer)***	- Voyager ***(voyajay)***
25)	Pouvir ***(puvah)***	- Eassayer ***(assayeh)***
26)	Rendre***(rondhr)***	- Remettre***(rmethr)***
27)	Rire***(reeh)***	- Moquer ***(mokhr)***
28)	Tenir***(teneer)***-	-Porter ***(pokhter)***
29)	Valoir ***(valua)***	- Coûter ***(keter)***
30)	Voir ***(vuar)***	-Regarder ***(rehardhr)***

Le leçon 35

Les Antonyms

Check the meanings in dictionary to understand the formation of the words

1) acquérir*(akeeyeh)* -céder *(sayday)*
2) aller *(allay)* - venire*(veneer)*
3) Connaître*(kuneth)* -ignorer*(ignorch0*
4) Courir *(kureer)* - ouvrer*(oovrer)*
5) Boire *(buar)* - sucer *(sookrer)*
6) Croire *(kuar)* - douter*(dooter)*
7) Dire *(deeh)* - demander*(deemanday)*
8) Dormir *(dohmee)* - lever*(leveh)*
9) Essuyer *(asyuyeh)* - tremper*(thaumpay)*
10) Écrire *(akreeh)* -grifonner*(greeheefonay*
11) Faire *(freh)* - défaire*(defeh)*
12) Finir *(feeneer)* - Commencer*(kmaunsay)*
13) Joindre *(juandr)* - disjoindre*(deesjuandr)*
14) Lire - *(leeh)* - Déchiffrer*(deshifrer)*
15) Mettre *(methr)* - disperser *(dispehsay)*
16) Mourir *(murir)* - Vivre*(veevr)*
17) Naître *(naithr)* - Mourir*(murir)*
18) Offrir *(ofreer)* - Receivoir*(recevuar)*
19) Parler *(pakhlay)* - Taire *(teh)*
20) Partir *(pakhteer)* - Voyager*(voyajeh)*
21) Pouvir *(puvah)* - Repugner*(repoonjneh)*
22) Rendrc*(rondhr)* - Prêter*(preteh)*
23) Rire *(reeh)* - Larmoyer *(lahmoyeh)*
24) Tenir *teneer)*- - Lâcher*(lashay)*
25) Valoir *(valua)* - Rapporter *(rapporhter)*